A Piece of the Pie

The Story of Customer Service at Publix

by Joseph W. Carvin

A Piece of the Pie
The Story of Customer Service at Publix

Copyright © 2005
Joseph W. Carvin

All rights reserved. No part of this book may
be reproduced in any form, except for the
inclusion of brief quotations in a review,
without written permission in writing from
the author.

Interior photographs
© 2005 by Publix Super Markets, Inc.

Printed in the U.S.A. by
Morris Publishing Co.
3212 East Highway 30
Kearney, NE 68847
1-800-650-7888

ISBN 0-9768183-0-2

A Piece
of the Pie

The Story of Customer Service at Publix

by Joseph W. Carvin

Foreword

This year marks the seventy-fifth anniversary of the Publix family. That's seventy-five years of doing our best to make Publix a place where "shopping is a pleasure."

Over the years, the Publix family has grown from a handful of people to well over a hundred thousand associates. I've watched them serve customers with a friendly enthusiasm that's difficult to describe. I've watched them go on to become Publix managers and to spread their own friendliness and enthusiasm to others. Their commitment to excellence always makes me proud. As I read through the stories in this book, I felt again and again how fortunate we've been at Publix to have such an incredible group of people as part of our Publix family.

Joe Carvin worked with Publix for twenty-five years – roughly, the quarter century since Publix's last major anniversary. In 1998, the Board of Directors elected Joe to manage the human resources function at Publix. For both of these reasons, he's in a good position to understand where Publix is today and how we got there.

Through this collection of real-life experiences from Publix customers and associates, Joe captures the heart of what Publix people are all about. These stories provide an insight into the spirit of Publix and our company's success.

To all who may read this book, I appreciate your interest in Publix. To our customers, I hope you'll enjoy reading about some of the things we do to make shopping a pleasure. And to Publix associates, I thank you for all you do each day for your customers and for each other. I encourage you to continue "writing the story" of Publix as you create real-life customer service stories every day.

Charlie Jenkins, Jr.
CEO
Publix Super Markets, Inc.

Table of Contents

Acknowledgement

I should acknowledge my personal bias. For the twenty-five years I worked with Publix people, first as an outside lawyer (what my lawyer friends like to call an "outhouse" lawyer) and eventually as the company's vice president of human resources, I went through a conversion from skeptical outsider to a real fan of the company. Now retired, I still own a "piece of the pie." And I'm still amazed at what I learned about the people of Publix.

So if you're looking for an objective appraisal of Publix, be forewarned. I believe that Publix is genuinely unique.

This book consists mostly of brief stories of real people and events which illustrate the points made. While some of the stories come from my personal experience, the vast majority are stories that others have shared with me. I want to thank those people at Publix – most notably Tina Johnson, Joe Schaefer, Jennifer Bush and Iris Stackpole – who helped me gather these stories and check facts. Even more, I want to thank all the many customers and associates of Publix who provided stories for the book.

Wherever possible, I have used *actual names* of both customers and associates. (In a few cases, names have been changed to protect privacy.) So I'm not going to list all those who made contributions; they appear throughout the pages that follow. But to each of you who took the time to share with me some part of your experience with Publix – either as an associate or as a customer – *thank you*! You are indeed incredible people.

PART ONE

"WHERE SHOPPING IS A PLEASURE"

1.
Spirit

*B*y 1993, Publix had reached the top of the charts in customer satisfaction ratings. It had just been named one of the top ten places to work in America. And I had recently become a full-time associate in its human resources department. I was in the office of Jim Rhodes, then vice president of human resources. The office was tastefully decorated with select pieces of Publix memorabilia, accumulated over Jim's thirty years of service with Publix. Jim was telling me a story from "the good old days" when he was a meat manager in a store. His eyes sparkled as he told me his story.

"It's my day off," said Jim, "and I'm mowing my lawn when my wife calls me to the phone. It's Joe Blanton (then the president of Publix) on the phone. Joe says he's just been on the phone with a customer. The customer's upset. Something about a Publix pizza ruining her oven. But he's not really sure what the problem is. He asks me to call her. So I do.

"She's very agitated," he goes on. "Ranting something about her oven being filthy. She's demanding to know what Publix is going to do about it. She's not really making a lot of sense, you know? So I suggest I come out to her house, so I can talk to her, face to face."

He continues.

"I wash up and put on a clean white shirt and a tie. I drive over to her house, on the beach. Her husband meets me at the door. He's got a dark tan and he's wearing several gold chains around his neck. (No shirt, just the tan.) His wife is decked out in an evening dress. She's still carrying on about Publix pizza ruining her oven.

"So I ask if I can see the oven. She shows me where it is. Let me tell you, there was so much blackened grease and cheese and garbage burnt into the walls of that oven – at least two and a half inches of it, all caked up and charred real good. I asked if she still had the box the pizza came in, and we read the instructions together.

"The instructions said to preheat the oven to 350 degrees and then put the pizza in the oven. They didn't say anything about using a baking pan. Come to find out, she hadn't used any kind of cooking sheet to catch the grease or the toppings. She'd put the pizza directly on the oven rack, just as she had with every other pizza she'd ever cooked in that oven. It was obvious what had happened. The toppings and grease had been coming off her pizza for years. And just as obvious, she hadn't ever cleaned the oven. It had finally gotten so bad it had caught fire."

Then Jim smiled.

"And still, she was demanding to know what Publix was going to do!"

"So what did you do?" I asked.

I didn't know anything about customer service. I was an employment lawyer. I was doing what I'd been trained to do: figuring out how the situation might look in court. The Publix Guarantee read, "If for any reason your purchase does not give you complete satisfaction, the full purchase price will be cheerfully refunded immediately upon request."

"Did you give the customer her money back?" I asked.

Jim looked at me with a patient smile. The kind of smile I often got at Publix. "Not exactly," he said.

Then Jim – who, like almost all Publix associates our age, was a life-long Publix associate – explained how he'd handled the situation.

"I explained to her why the fire had started," said Jim. "She was a little embarrassed, but I made sure she didn't feel too bad about it. Then I told her to hold on, I'd be right back. I went to my store. When I came back, I had two pizzas and a baking pan. I also had a putty scraper and four or five cans of oven cleaner. I gave her the pizzas and the baking pan. Then I rolled up my sleeves, got down on my knees, and cleaned out her oven for her. I polished it until it looked like new."

My mouth, usually so full of "on the one hand this, and on the other hand, that," hung open. I didn't know what to make of Jim's lesson. It made no sense to me. I was used to thinking about people's rights and obligations. After years of neglect, Jim had no obligation to clean this customer's oven. And his story raised a big question of business efficiency. Going out to this customer's house in the first place seemed unnecessary – surely, he had better things to do with his time.

I'd spent fourteen years at that point recording my time in minutes for billing purposes. (I'd been taught to divide hours into tenths, billing my clients for every six-minute interval.) Surely, if Jim had asked the woman to bring the pizza back to the store for a refund, she would have been satisfied. For Jim to go out to the woman's house – to spend several hours of his day off, cleaning her oven – it seemed nothing short of crazy to me!

But the pride with which Jim told me his story was obvious. And there was something about the way he'd said "my" store that I couldn't miss. I was beginning to see the impact of what can happen when someone "owns a piece of the pie."

But more on that later. Let's not get ahead of the story.

Publix Super Markets is the largest employee-owned company in the United States – and probably in the world. It employs over 120,000 associates (not "employees" – more on that later, too) in over eight hundred stores spread across five states. To supply these stores, it has the largest truck fleet in the state of Florida, carrying groceries daily from some of the largest distribution centers in the world. It now serves well over a million customers every day. Yet, despite its growth from Florida into four other southeastern states, after seventy-five years in business, some say it still has the feel of a small mom-and-pop grocery store. It's consistently rated at the top of the industry in customer satisfaction and financial performance. And in 1993, it had just been named by Robert Levering and Milton Moscowitz as one of the top ten best companies to work for in America.[1]

An average Publix store sells over twenty million dollars of groceries a year. To do this, it's open seven days a week throughout the year (closed only on Easter, Thanksgiving, and Christmas day). Most stores receive at least one tractor trailer load of inventory a day (or night), often more.

You've been in a supermarket at all hours of the day. At most stores, there's merchandise moving through the checkout lanes pretty fast. Well, for every item going out the front door, there's an item coming in the back door – at pretty much the same speed and over pretty much the same span of hours. The store turns that inventory over by serving about three thousand customers a day. That's about a million customers going through the check out lanes every year, at each store.

The store is open seven days a week. Open to the public at 7 a.m., a store that's going to have fresh bread for its morning customers needs people starting work in the bakery well before

---

[1] In Chapter 10 of *The One Hundred Best Companies to Work for in America*, Currency/Doubleday, 1993.

dawn. And staying open until 11 p.m., with some truck deliveries after midnight, a store that wants to be clean the next morning often needs people mopping floors or unloading trucks after midnight the night before. Publix associates are working on Memorial Day and Labor Day and the Fourth of July.

At the same time, stiff competition and thin profit margins in the grocery industry mean that profits average less than two cents on every sales dollar. That means that if a single item is lost or damaged, the store must sell fifty more of that same item to recover the loss and break even.

And customers are in a big hurry.

To compete in this kind of business, the average Publix store employs about a hundred and forty people. Larger stores employ over three hundred. And like all jobs, a job in a retail store can be stressful.

It's easy to imagine how such a busy atmosphere might lead to tension or stress. In such an environment, it could be easy to lose sight of what's important. Yet Publix has been nationally rated "number one" in customer satisfaction by virtually every rating entity in the business.

On Christmas Eve, 2003, the company received the following e-mail through its website:

> I've been shopping at your Silver Lakes store for several years, and have always had a positive experience. Your store is much cleaner, better stocked, and the checkout lines move much more quickly than the competitor's store next door. The reason I am writing this note is to inform you of an incident I observed regarding one of your associates, Michael McDougall. My wife and I were parked next to a woman who treated your employee in the worst possible manner. This was perhaps the worst I have ever witnessed. Mr. McDougall was insulted, berated, and dismissed.
>
> Your employee composed himself without indication of frustration. He turned toward myself and my wife and wished us a good evening. Your employee's composure was nothing less than extraordinary. Great job!
>
> How can I get my employees to treat the public this way?
>> Scott Killian
>> Pembroke Pines, Florida

With this book, I attempt to answer Mr. Killian's question.

Of course, customer satisfaction comes from many things: variety and quality of products, clean stores, and fair prices are high on the list. The physical aspects of the store – fixtures, lighting, high ceilings, bright colors, wide aisles – all play an important part. Some customers rave about product quality, freshness and selection. To make Publix a place "where shopping is a pleasure," there has to be all of these things. But this book will have a narrower focus.

To answer Mr. Killian's question, "How can I get my employees to treat the public this way?" this book will focus on only one element of customer satisfaction: customer service. That is, it will concentrate on the people in the organization, and what they do and why.

I'll first set out more specifically *what* Publix's acclaimed service consists of – "what the fuss is all about." To do this, I've talked to numerous Publix customers and analyzed several hundred customer letters which explain, in the customers' own words, what it is they find so impressive about the service at Publix.

Then I'll turn to the business practices which foster this kind of service at Publix. I'll explain how I believe Mr. Killian can get *his* employees to treat the public this way – and how I believe others like him can do the same in their businesses.

The story of Publix began in Winter Haven, Florida, in 1930...

...and continues with stores like this one inBirmingham, Alabama, which opened in June 2003.

2.

Customer Response: a Sample

*W*hat *is* customer service at Publix?
What is it that customers find worth raving about?

I asked Clayton Hollis (Publix's vice president of public affairs) to send me comments that the consumer relations department had received from Publix customers. These would be people who weren't simply satisfied with their shopping experience, but who got home from the grocery store and sat down and took the time to call, e-mail, or write a letter to Publix about it. To use the phrase popularized by Sheldon Bowles and Ken Blanchard, these would be "raving fans" of Publix. By looking at what they say, we can get a look at what sets Publix apart.

The consumer relations department sent comments that had been posted by customers on the company's website – www.publix.com – during a period of eight weeks in the final quarter of 2003. They described what Publix does to create customer enthusiasm and loyalty.

Let's look at a few of these postings. The names and details here are all real, as described by the customers and Publix associates involved.

From one of Publix's newest markets in Tennessee, the first comment was about initiative:

> I thought service was dead. I visited your store in Hendersonville twice this week, looking for a particular item. I wasn't sure what it was called, but the staff was very keen in helping me locate it. They did not wait for me to approach them for help, they sought me out... Patrick O'Connor asked me if he could help me find anything... We looked for a few moments and he called Scott over to help, who was able to retrieve the exact type of "nut" I was looking for from the back. Just the fact that these people didn't allow me to go to them for help was very refreshing.
>
> I worked retail management for over ten years, but I got out due to the inability of the company I worked for to take care of customers. If I ever decide to get back into

retail, I will go to work for Publix. You have my business and support.

Spencer Holman
Gallatin, Tennessee

From a store in Publix's home town of Lakeland, Florida, there was a comment about helpfulness: Shubhangi Thorat wrote that as Thanksgiving approached, she'd decided to cook an exotic Indian meal for her co-workers. She picked up two packages of legs and thighs. She was wondering how she was going to cut them into small pieces when a store associate walked over. When she asked him if he'd be willing to cut the pre-packaged chicken up into small pieces, his response was "Sure. *How small do you want the pieces?*"

"I asked if there was a charge," she wrote. "I was most willing to pay for it. He replied in the negative. So I asked him if he would cut a whole turkey into small pieces for me – and he said "YES!"

Ms. Thorat was obviously impressed.

The next comment was about clean stores and friendliness:

I visited [Store 648] on November 29 and was amazed by [Kevin Kellogg's] graciousness. I had just put the kids in the bench cart when he came over, bent down and began a friendly conversation with my children. Throughout the store the employees were helpful, smiling and pleasant. The store was immaculate and well organized.

As I was checking out, my daughter was helping put items on the belt, and she dropped an entire gallon of milk in the lane. I was so embarrassed but he [Kevin] comes right over and begins to help clean up the mess. My daughter felt bad about what had happened, so he tries to cheer her up by offering her a balloon. He then kindly pushes our cart to the car and proceeds to unload our groceries for us.

I'm not sure how he can have a store that looks great, employees smiling, and still have time for incredible customer service. I'm appreciative. Thank you.

C. S.
Fort Myers, Florida

On December 8th, the website received a compliment about

carry-out service – specifically, a front service clerk (bagger) known to the customer only as "Becky." First, Becky greeted the customer politely and helped her with her coupons. ("All together, she saved me about ten dollars!") Then:

> ... she insisted on carrying my groceries to my car. She talked to me the whole way. As I drove away, I passed her collecting carts in the parking lot. She looked at me and waved and said, 'Have a nice day.'
> *It was like I was in one of your commercials!*
> Emily Dockery
> Orlando, Florida

Two days later, customer Mary Duff complimented Del Cragin of the Hunter's Creek Publix. Why? She'd wanted three 12-packs of cupcakes for her son's birthday party at school. The store didn't have three 12-packs, but Del gave her one 12-pack and four 6-packs for the same price, and was remarkably friendly while doing so. "He totally impressed me," she said, "*and I felt like I was really getting the service and quality that you advertise on TV.*"

Another comment was about extra effort in problem-solving:

The problem: Kristin Schnell's husband wanted to get a bottle opener that played the Georgia Fight Song. He'd told her he'd seen one for sale and wanted to get it as a Christmas present for a neighbor who was a "Dawg's" fan. Ms. Schnell searched the Publix store in Clermont one evening but couldn't find the Dawg's bottle opener.

The first effort: When the customer went to check out, a cashier, Natalie Sperling, asked her if she had found everything she wanted. She admitted she hadn't, and mentioned the musical bottle openers.

The second effort: Since Natalie didn't know whether any of the musical bottle openers were left, she asked one of the managers on duty. The manager said he hadn't seen any of them in months.

Disappointed, the customer proceeded to check out with the rest of her groceries. But as she was leaving the store, Natalie came running up to her. She was carrying one of the musical bottle openers. It was the last one.

"Where in the world did you find it?" asked Ms. Schnell, having searched the entire store herself.

"In the frozen food aisle."

16

Frozen Foods is not the first place a person would look for a musical bottle opener. It was obvious to the customer that Natalie had searched the entire store. *A successful third effort.*

"I was so surprised that, even after I had taken no for an answer, she continued looking for this bottle opener," wrote Ms. Schnell. "Obviously, Natalie had made it her mission to satisfy me – and she succeeded. "

There was another compliment about extra helpfulness:

> I stopped in the store this morning on the way to work to have thirty balloons blown up for a co-worker's birthday. Two men took care of blowing them up, bagging, etc. I didn't realize how much space thirty balloons would take up in my car (a Beetle) and when we realized I would not be able to drive safely with them all jammed in my car, one of the men put balloons in his truck and drove to my office with me, even helping me in the doors of the building with all the balloons! They couldn't have been nicer and more helpful! Thank you so much!
>
> Joann Spiers
> Marietta, Georgia

Another comment was about extra service after a mishap: Margot Watson had bought some things for a food drive – on a Thursday – and left them in the trunk of her car. On Sunday, opening her trunk, she found that one of the bags was no longer in the net she uses to keep groceries from rolling around. Unfortunately, the bag had contained a gallon jug of laundry detergent. The detergent had come out, had fallen to its side, and had been rolling around in the trunk of her car for three days. It was nearly empty, having leaked out all over her car.

Ms. Watson returned the almost empty bottle to the store and told a manager – Paul DiPietrantonio – what had happened. Then, Ms. Watson showed Paul the trunk of her car.

After apologizing for the mess, Paul took the carpeting out of the trunk and rinsed and cleaned it for her.

"I am a widow and live in a condo with no facilities for this kind of washing," wrote Ms. Watson. "I have not particularly liked Publix prior to this, but this puts a completely different light on things…"

Of course, sometimes service isn't what it ought to be, and not every posting on the website is a positive one. On November 28, John Anderson used the website to express his disappointment. He'd been told by clerks in Sarasota that Publix's store brand natural peanut butter had been discontinued. He posted his comments to let the corporate office know of his disappointment.

The following day, John was astounded when a Publix assistant store manager, Melody Pruitt, knocked on the door of his home. She explained that the clerks didn't have the full story – yes, the original supplier's product had been discontinued (because of a problem with leaking seals). But a new supplier had been found and Publix natural peanut butter was still available. In fact, in light of the misunderstanding, she had brought two jars of the peanut butter with her.

John was so impressed that Melody would come to his home with the product that he posted another message the following day: "I am very grateful for the interest Publix has shown in an individual customer. THANK YOU VERY MUCH!"

John later described how he'd told the story many times, "to friends, acquaintances, and even strangers... The personalized response we got from Publix deserves to be recognized!"

With those nine customer letters, we get our first look at the service that causes customers to write. According to this small sample, what constitutes service "worth writing to Publix about" includes:

- Excellent food choices
- Clean, well-organized stores
- Carry-out service
- Initiative – helping customers find product
- Helpfulness – cutting pre-packaged meat
- Extra effort (driving balloons to the customer's office)
- Extra service after mishaps (like spilled detergent in the trunk)
- Courtesy and graciousness (cheering up an upset child)
- Friendliness
- Personal recognition and attention

3.
Digging Deeper

*O*f course, lots of companies get letters from satisfied customers. I know of no formal study that says Publix gets more such letters than most. But consider:

In 1993, Publix was included in the "top ten" list in the book, *The One Hundred Best Companies to Work for in America.*[2]

In the same year, a national consumer magazine reported Publix at the top of a reader survey on customer satisfaction.

In 1995, The *New York Times* ran a feature titled "Shopping Purgatory or Paradise." It was subtitled "Northeast's Supermarkets Outclassed by Sun Belt's." The article compared Publix rather favorably to a "northern" super market in affluent Westchester County, New York:

> A supermarket run by the Publix chain in a middle-class neighborhood in Lakeland, Florida, offered a startling contrast: clutter-free, wide-aisled, spotless and with employees given to friendly chatter and small courtesies. Not only were there grocery baggers, but they asked, "Can I help you out to your car with this?" and then loaded customers' automobiles, declining tips. Instead of staying at the registers, idle checkers ranged into the aisles to urge shoppers into their lanes.[3]

In 1995, the American Customer Satisfaction Index (ACSI) rated Publix with the highest score, not only in the nation's super market industry, but of any retailer in the country.[4]

In 1996, another survey by a nationwide consumer magazine ranked Publix America's favorite supermarket.

---

[2] *The One Hundred Best Companies to Work for in America,* Currency/ Doubleday, 1993

[3] New York Times, April 25, 1995. Shopping Purgatory or Paradise, by Glenn Collins.

[4] The ACSI is based on customer evaluations of the quality of products and services available in the United States. It is produced by a partnership of the University of Michigan Business School, American Society for Quality and CFI Group.

In 1998, Publix was named "Retailer of the Year" by *Progressive Grocer* magazine.

In 2001, Publix was one of PlanetFeedback's "A-Rated Companies" for customer satisfaction.

In the September, 2003 issue of *Florida Monthly* magazine, a reader survey named Publix "Best Grocery Store."

In 2004, *for the 10th year in a row,* Publix earned the highest consumer ranking of any retailer in the nation, according to the ACSI.

And in January of 2005, Publix was included in FORTUNE magazine's "Hall of Fame," having been recognized by that magazine as one of the country's best places to work *for eight consecutive years.*

In short, it's not just my biased perception that Publix delivers superior service. It's hard to argue with objective measures like these. Like any company, Publix sometimes disappoints. But the independent ratings listed here reflect something about customer satisfaction at Publix. And this customer satisfaction has continued, year after year, to fuel Publix's growth and the value of its stock.

Consider: In 1979, the company had just over two hundred stores. By the end of 2003, it had over eight hundred. This growth was not from the purchase of other companies, but from the building of additional stores and the gaining of new customers, one at a time. In that same period, Publix grew from about 25,000 associates to over 125,000 – by hiring and training people, one at a time. And on May 1, 2004, while the rest of the stock market was sluggish and most other food retailers were suffering, Publix's stock price hit an all time high. As of that date, with dividends reinvested, a hundred dollars of stock bought in 1959 (when the company's current stock purchase plan was begun) was worth $138,802.

Also in 2004, Publix surpassed Safeway, becoming the top-ranked supermarket in the nation on FORTUNE magazine's list of most admired companies.[5]

One of the best places to work. Tops in customer satisfaction. Admired by its peers.

My appetite whetted, I wanted to be sure I understood what really caused customers to rave. As the comments continued to come in, my understanding started to grow.

---

[5] FORTUNE magazine, March 8, 2004.

From Clearwater came a letter raving about the friendly service at Store 867:

I have served 16 years in the customer service industry. I have seen many lectures about exemplary customer service. It is rare to experience this type of service while grocery shopping or going to a local restaurant; I experience this type of service when I am paying top dollar having brunch at the Ritz Carlton. This Publix store exhibited top notch customer service skills and then some. It should be video-taped and sent out across the nation to all types of 'What It Takes to Serve Your Customer' seminars. I pray that you will take the time to somehow applaud what they did right.

J. D.
Clearwater, Florida

From Tampa came another:

The food was top notch, but the people you had preparing it and dealing with me were the stars. When represented by this store, Publix is shown as the best quality, the best staffed, the cleanest and the overall best store in Tampa ... of ANY store, not just Publix. These guys were fantastic.

J. R.
Tampa, Florida

This simple letter was received by Tom Bradley in Clermont:

Comments:
On the day March 20 at 9:30, I was impressed of a employee there that bagged my grocery. I am not sure what his name was but I think it was edwin or edward but he was short and had a hat. He was kind to me and my wife help us in a aisle to find tomato paste. He even took us out to the car I wanted to give him a tip for his hard work but he would not take it so I was wondering if you might give that boy a little something as my thanks he really did a wonderful job keep up the good work.

J. S.
Clermont, Florida

As I reviewed stacks of letters from customers, one of the first things I noticed was that many of the comments didn't seem to be about the buying and selling of groceries. For example, from Homewood, Alabama, came the following:

ARE YOU
MISSING ME?
Found here at Publix
January 1,2004
Contact Shele at
Publix Customer Service.
Or Call 205-944-1101

Along with the picture came a note: the lost dog's owner had looked for *Precious* for two days before finally coming upon the above poster at Publix. The happy customer explained that the store "had really gotten him out of the doghouse" with his wife!

A few days later, customer Kathy Kordana wrote about when she first moved to Lakeland. It had been late one evening – only fifteen minutes before closing time – that she walked into a Publix for the first time. After shopping a few aisles she noticed someone was mopping the floors. When a manager approached, she expected to be asked to finish up and check out. Instead, the manager told her to take her time and finish her shopping. Then, turning to the guy with the mop, the manager asked him to re-mop the areas Ms. Kordana had already been through. Ms. Kordana wrote that she's been a customer ever since.

Another customer sent a letter about Store 559 in Kennesaw, Georgia. That Sunday afternoon, she'd brought an armful of used plastic bags to the store for recycling. She'd deposited her bags into the recycling bin outside the store, then left. But at 8:30 that evening, she discovered that her diamond ring was missing. All she could think was the worst: it must have slipped off her finger and gone into the recycling bin with the bags!

The customer was terrified at the thought of the bin being emptied, her ring hauled off to the shredding plant somewhere miles away. It had been several hours since she deposited her bags. At 8:45 p.m., she called the store and got Bonnie Mykytyn. It was nearly closing time.

Bonnie informed her that a truck had just left the store, and the first thing she wanted to do was to see if the truck had picked up the recyclables.

"She called me back twenty minutes later and told me that she had found my ring," wrote the customer. "She had gone through all the bags and searched until she found it... I had expected her to hold the bags for me to search through the next day."

There it was. Exceeding the customer's expectations.

"She told me she would put the ring in the safe until I could come by the next morning. Needless to say, I slept well that night thanks to Bonnie's efforts."

Sophia Allen posted a message to the website. She had been shopping at a Publix in Palm Harbor while seven months pregnant. When she lost her purse, she started crying hysterically in the middle of the store. ("Pregnancy hormones" she wrote.) The store crew started searching the store, and came up with nothing. Then they spent about three hours examining security video tapes, hoping for a clue. At the same time, they helped her contact authorities and – she stressed in the letter of thanks she wrote the company – they comforted her with *hugs*.

Hugs?

The purse was eventually recovered. Not only that, Ms. Allen delivered a healthy baby boy.

"I was so thankful," said Sophia. "I'll forever be a Publix shopper."

4.

The Purple Potato Perspective

*A*s I reviewed the customer comments I'd received, one in particular caught my attention. A customer had posted a comment on the Publix website about purple potatoes:

> Last week, James in the produce department overheard one of my comments to a stock clerk about "purple potatoes" and he suggested I try a local organic store for them. He also suggested that I give him my name and phone number so that he could check on the item for me. I tried for a week phoning *every* produce market and vegetable stand from Jacksonville to Tampa to find someone who knew what a purple potato was and where I could get some. This morning, James at the Oviedo store, #329, called and said the purple potatoes were in.
>
> One big "Way to go!" to the staff at my Publix on Alapha Woods!
>
> B. D.
Oviedo, Florida

Purple potatoes?

I had no idea what a "purple potato" was. As I thought it over, the question began to fester: Was I *qualified* to write a book about the retail food business?

As I mulled over the purple potato, I came to the sad conclusion that as a lawyer, I'd been living in a different world. A world where everything was a shade of gray. A world *without* purple potatoes!

After all, most lawyers don't know anything about customer service. And I didn't know the difference between a rump roast and a brisket of – what do they call those things?

To penetrate to the essence, I'd need to go to the source: retail people. To learn not only what Publix's customers had to say, but what Publix's own managers and sales clerks and front-service clerks (baggers) had to say.

And so I asked Publix to help me collect experiences and insights from Publix associates. Publix spent several months at the beginning of 2004 collecting comments from Publix people.

Current associates shared their experiences and insights about how they viewed customer service, and why they performed as they did.

As I read their e-mails and spoke to many of them, the picture fell into place, piece by piece. It was a picture I'd been looking at for twenty-five years, but now that I'd focused on it so closely, it knocked my socks off.

Unfortunately, not all their stories can be included here. But Publix's recipe for success can't be understood without understanding the way Publix associates think, and there's no better way than to hear stories of customer service from people who do know what a purple potato is.

There's one former associate to consider first: the *first* Publix associate. The *original*. Publix's founder, Mr. George Jenkins.

No conversation at Publix can go long without somebody referring to "Mr. George." The reference to him isn't always a reference to his name; sometimes, it's the use of a word or a phrase or advice he once gave. But Mr. George is everywhere at Publix. His picture hangs in its warehouses, its manufacturing plants, and in its stores. His face looks out over Publix's people as if to remind them of his commitments: to them, and to the customer. Publix's success cannot be understood without reference to Mr. George.

To retell the story of Publix's humble beginnings, Mr. George was only 17 years old – not long out of high school – when he moved to Florida with $9 in his pocket. He got a job as a stock clerk at a Piggly Wiggly store in Tampa, where he made $15 a week. The Piggly Wiggly store was part of a franchise operation, one of fourteen stores owned by the same man. George worked hard and let his natural friendliness do the rest. Five years later, he was managing the owner's largest store in Winter Haven. Then the franchise was sold.

The new owner never visited his stores. Having some issues he wanted to discuss, George made a trip to see the man in Atlanta. The story is often told of what happened next. In Mr. George's own words:

> I went to see my absentee boss and he sent out word that he was in an important conference and could not be disturbed. Well, I could hear what that conference was all about. He was talking about his last golf game. Right then I resolved that if I ever got to be a big shot in this business, two things would be done: I'd go around and visit the

stores, and if anybody wanted to see me they could walk into my office any time.

Returning to Winter Haven, I turned in my apron, took the money I had saved to buy a new car, about $1,300, and in 1930, opened my own store next to the one I'd left.

So it was that Publix began.

Mr. George had a basic concept about customers. In those days, the customer (nearly always a woman) walked in, told the clerk what she wanted, and waited for the clerk to gather her order from the shelves. (The clerk often had to climb a ladder to do so.) As the customer waited, there was ample opportunity for chit chat between the customer and the grocer. Grocery clerks and customers got to know each other. Personal relationships developed.

Meanwhile stores were opening elsewhere in the country where customers were expected to collect their own groceries. Piggly Wiggly and Kroger were trying out the concept of "self-service." In 1930, the same year Mr. George opened the first Publix, Michael Cullen opened the first "King Kullen" store in Queens, New York. It was among the first high volume "super markets," where the idea of self-service allowed the store to keep its payroll to a minimum, and prices low. Some of the new northern supermarkets were cramming as much product as possible into the store, their whole focus being on driving prices down by driving volume up.

Mr. George took a similar tack on price, but a different one altogether on service. By adopting the self-service model and aiming for high volume, he, too, could drive prices down. But as important as product and price were, nothing, in the end, was as important as the customer's shopping experience. In 1940, he closed his old grocery stores (by that time, there were two of them) and opened a real *supermarket*.

The book *Fifty Years of Pleasure*, published on the occasion of Publix's 50th anniversary, tells some of the things Mr. George did. He'd seen an electric eye door on a trip to New York, and it occurred to him that customers might appreciate not having to open the door manually – he was the first to put them in his store. Though air-conditioning was still all but unheard-of, he installed an air conditioning system. He replaced the old dark shelving with bright displays, and added fluorescent lighting. He was among the first retail merchants to add running water in his store, to supply a fountain at which the customer could get a cool drink while shopping. In an age when customers of other stores nearly always had to find parking spaces on the street, he made sure *his* store had its own parking lot.

He was going all out to give meaning to a new word in the English language. Seventy five years later, we tend to run the syllables together, in a single word: *supermarket*. We forget that when the word was new, it was two words, meant to stress how special the new-fangled places would be: *super* markets. To this day, Publix retains the two-word version in its name: Publix *Super Markets*, Inc.

Meanwhile, as much as Mr. George recognized the benefits of "mass merchandising," he saw a danger. He worried that a customer who'd been left to select groceries on her own might quickly lose personal contact with the grocer. Mr. George wanted to maintain that direct contact, that *person-to-person relationship* with the customer. In other words, while he was modern enough to see the benefits of mass merchandising, he was old-fashioned enough to understand that people are happiest when they're in the company of friends.

Mr. George feared that self-service and "supermarkets" could drive the sales clerk and the customer apart. He resolved to keep that from happening -- to keep the personal touch in his stores. If his customers were going to wander around a large store collecting their own groceries, what would he have to do, to make sure the customer felt personally *cared about*, as a fellow human being?

It was not until 1949 that Mr. George hired Bill Schroter, and it was Bill Schroter who came up with the Publix slogan, "Where Shopping is a Pleasure." But that slogan simply captured the heart of what Mr. George had already determined. From the beginning, the "customer coming first" at Publix was not simply about customer satisfaction with a product or a price, but customer *pleasure* while shopping in a Publix store.

5.

Honesty

*I*n March of 2004, a customer dropped a one hundred dollar bill on the check stand where his groceries were being bagged. It slipped under the bags. The customer was unaware he'd dropped the bill. Front service clerk Matt Martin saw it and, without hesitation, handed the bill back to the customer. When the customer tried to give Matt a $20 reward, Matt declined it. The customer sent an e-mail to corporate, raving about Matt's honesty.

Ms. Betty Williams wrote about her experiences at the Monument Point store in Jacksonville:

> I have been shopping at Publix in Jacksonville for over 30 years. It is *very apparent to me that employee honesty and integrity is a top priority at Publix.* I have had three encounters at Publix that put my faith back into people.
>
> First, I left my ATM card in the machine, and all Bert had to do was hit another transaction and get whatever he wanted. But instead, he ran me down and returned my card. Thanks, Bert!
>
> Second, three twenty-dollar bills fell out of my pocket and one of the stock crew (I don't know who) returned the money. Can you believe this? I just called on a whim, not thinking anyone would turn in unidentifiable cash. Kudos to that person!
>
> And last but not least, I left a little denim change purse that was found by Tom Dean. No name, no phone number, no address, just $70.15 in cash. I thought this could not be happening. So what did I do? Call good old Publix one more time. And lo and behold, my change purse with the $70.15 was all there.
>
> God bless you Mr. Dean and the entire Publix crew. You all have restored my faith in mankind.
>
> Betty Williams
Jacksonville, Florida

In Evans, a purse found in a shopping cart out in the parking lot was delivered to the customer's home. In Port St. Lucie, a seventeen year old front service clerk found a diamond and ruby ring in the parking lot – and turned it in at the front desk. In Bradenton, front service clerk Floyd Brown found a check stub and over four hundred dollars in cash in the parking lot as he was gathering carts. The money was returned to the customer intact. And in Hialeah, manager Fred Catapano drove to a customer's home to return a wallet. The elderly man was afraid to answer the door, so Fred left him a note to come see him at the store to retrieve his wallet.

Over thirty years ago, then president Joe Blanton was asked what he looked for in selecting people to work at Publix. "Integrity, morals, honesty would be the top qualifications," he replied. "You have to be knowledgeable about your job, but I would rather have a man who knew nothing about his job but have him honest and moral. Then he could learn the job." That attitude about associate honesty has persisted at Publix to the present day.

At Store 106 in Fort Lauderdale, a wallet was found with over seven hundred dollars in it. The only other contents were a Canadian driver's license and a business card from a local motel. Larry Cole says the store called the motel only to be told the customer had already checked out. They were about to call the police to report the lost wallet when, as a last resort, *they called the motel back a second time*. Why? "To leave our information, in case the customer called back," says Larry. Sure enough, when they called the motel a second time, the customer had already returned, and was frantically searching the room and the hotel grounds for her wallet.

In January, 2004, the *Saint Augustine Record* ran a front page story about Chris Swanson, a sixteen-year-old Publix bagger, who'd found a purse in the Publix parking lot on New Year's Eve and turned it in – along with $3,000 in cash.

These stories should confirm an obvious point: honesty with customers is an essential element of customer service. But these days, the very fact that "honesty" plays so obvious a role might cause us to take it for granted, to give it insufficient thought. Sure, being honest is the right thing to do. Sure, if a customer finds an organization being *dis*honest, the customer will likely be lost forever. But rightly or wrongly, many customers these days perceive honesty to be the exception rather than the rule. The customer letters about honesty make clear that customers perceive honesty in the face of temptation to be *unusual*.

What this means is that when customers *experience* honesty, they are moved to take the time to write about it. As we'll see with other aspects of customer service, things that become "the norm" are soon taken for granted. It is those things that are *out of* the ordinary – the *extra* ordinary – that make the biggest impressions on customers. And for better or for worse, these days, customers view honesty as *extra*-ordinary.

Honesty, therefore, is the first ingredient of Publix's recipe for superior customer service.

6.
More Than a Guarantee

*A*fter honesty, the first notable ingredient in Publix's recipe for service is the Publix Guarantee. It's been around since Publix's earliest days.

Publix Guarantee

"We will never, knowingly, disappoint you. If for any reason your purchase does not give you complete satisfaction, the full purchase price will be cheerfully refunded immediately upon request."

There are many times Publix customers have been given refunds, based on the Guarantee. But in the many hundreds of customer letters Publix shared with me, there wasn't a single one in which a customer wrote to express thanks or to rave about getting a purchase price refunded. The Publix Guarantee is, itself, one of those things that has become the norm, and is now taken for granted. While it may be an essential ingredient for "satisfactory" service, the Guarantee is not an ingredient of "superior" service.

But there's something a little different about the Publix Guarantee. Whenever it's printed, it's followed by another sentence – a sentence that might, at first, seem almost an afterthought:

We have always believed that no sale is complete until the meal is eaten and enjoyed.

Mark Hollis, president of Publix between 1983 and 1995, tells of an experience he had in 1959.

"I had just been promoted to store manager at 'old number 28' in Largo, Florida," he says. "I was a self confident (some said cocky) twenty-five year old who really thought he had all the answers. A customer came in one morning with a package of cottage cheese that was spoiled and out of date. I apologized and took the container out of the bag and immediately noticed that it was a 'Super Brand' label – a product of the Winn-Dixie Company.

"'Oh!' I said, 'I'm so sorry but this is a Winn-Dixie product. We don't sell that brand.'

"She responded very nicely, "Goodness me, I forgot -- my husband did say he stopped by Winn-Dixie the other day to pick up something for me. That's okay, I'll just go back there to exchange it.'

"As she walked out the door – headed for my competitor's store – I stood there feeling like an imbecile. I actually gave her a reason to go to another store! But my lesson was now ingrained in my brain. The customer may not always be right, but my job was to *make the situation feel right* for the customer."

There it was. The distinction I'd been having such a hard time understanding.

Being right is one thing. Making someone else *feel* right is another.

"Our main responsibility should be to help customers have a better day," says office cashier Douglas Atkins. "This is what we do at Publix."

Let's take a closer look at how Publix people deal with the additional statement. The *afterthought*: "We have always believed that no sale is complete until the meal is eaten and enjoyed."

One customer went to a store in Nokomis to pick up food, balloons, cake and supplies she'd ordered for her daughter's birthday party – only to find that her cake was not ready. At first, someone in the bakery told her the cake would be ready within the hour. But being still nervous, she went to speak to Jennifer Kline, the store manager. Jennifer could see that Publix wasn't meeting the customer's needs.

"I had barely spoken a few words," the customer later wrote to Publix president Ed Crenshaw, "when she said they would *deliver* the cake by 11 a.m. I was blown away..."

Another customer, on Marco Island, had been promised that a fruit basket would be ready by noon on Friday. When he arrived at Store 622 to pick it up at 3 p.m., he was distraught that no one knew about the order. Assistant store manager Tina Johnson confirmed the company's error.

"She told me, 'You go home and I'll have the basket delivered within the hour, free of charge,'" wrote the customer. "It was my feeling that 'free of charge' meant that there would be no charge for the delivery – for which I would have felt grateful. When I asked if I could pay for the basket now in order to save time, she said, 'No, I meant *the basket* will be free of charge.'

"I was totally flabbergasted... Ms. Johnson took what was a big disappointment for me, but knew exactly what to do to insure my continued satisfaction with Publix. Less than forty minutes later, the basket arrived at my door, and it was truly beautiful ..."

Tina had demonstrated the art of turning disappointment into delight.

At Publix, genuine *beliefs*, like the belief that "the sale isn't complete until the meal is eaten and enjoyed," drive actions to please the customer. To those with a service mentality, the idea that a sale "isn't complete until the meal has been eaten and enjoyed" has nothing to do with concepts like "fault" or "blame." It's about making the customer feel good.

As Publix president Ed Crenshaw says, "We never want our customers to leave our stores disappointed for any reason. We know we're being taken advantage of at times. But as Mr. George always said, 'If you take care of the product, it won't come back; if you take care of the customer, they'll always come back.' It's a very simple philosophy that I believe our managers really understand."

Consider this: a customer in Marietta was in the parking lot unloading his cart when the door of his van came back and slammed his funny bone – causing him to drop a 12-pack of Coke, sending the soda spewing and flying in all directions. The customer was furious at himself, and kicked the van door in frustration. A young front service clerk, seventeen-year-old Kevin McFelia, noticed the customer's frustration and approached with an offer of help.

"Let me help you with that, sir," he said. And then the zinger: "I'll go and get you another 12-pack."

The customer remarked that the young man's courtesy and service went "far beyond anything I have seen in a long, long time." How many times had I seen the signs in other retail stores: "You break it, you buy it." This was almost the reverse of that. Legally, once a sale is made, once the customer leaves the register with the product, the product belongs to the customer. If the product slips and breaks, well, too bad, so sad! For a retailer to *replace* the product that gets damaged *after* it leaves the store? Entirely unnecessary. *But* – the meal hadn't yet been eaten or enjoyed!

One afternoon, two managers in Madeira Beach, John Kendall and Brandie Haley, were walking back to their store from the middle school across the street, when they noticed a car accident on the corner. The occupants of the cars were standing on the median, looking distraught. The managers noticed that the crushed trunk of one of the cars had Publix grocery bags in it – in sorry shape, of course. These managers understood how stressful a traffic accident can be – certainly no way to end a day's shopping at Publix. And they *believed* that the sale is not complete until the meal is eaten and enjoyed. After making sure the occupants were all okay, the managers told the customer he could come back to the store any time and replace the damaged groceries, free of charge.

"The customer's once white and distraught face turned into a smile," says Brandie Haley. *Mission accomplished.*

Pat Miskar, a cake decorator at the Bayonet Point store, got a call after selling a birthday cake. The customer had gotten home and put the cake – intended for her son's birthday – on her dining room table. Without her knowledge, her two rottweilers had been watching her, and as soon as her back was turned, the rottweilers had decided to check out the cake for themselves. The cake was destroyed. The party was that night, and the customer was delighted when Pat said she could have another cake decorated in time for the party.

But when the customer arrived to pick up the second cake, she was still clearly stressed out from having an especially rough day. So Pat gave her the second cake for free.

"The customer left the store happy," says Pat.

In the end, it seemed, that was what mattered.

Natalie Baltra tells the following story about her store manager, Brian Singletary:

A teacher from Mitchell High School was in shopping one afternoon. When she got home, as she was walking through her utility room, her plastic bag broke and the glass jar of olive oil spilled all over her linoleum floor. The oil was tracked all over her carpet. She was a single parent of two children with just enough money to get by on, and was trying to get dinner made up for the family when she called to talk to the store manager. She was clearly upset.

Mr. Singletary got two part-timers and gathered up

some cleaning products and headed over to the woman's house. When they got there, they started the clean up. Mr. Singletary was on his hands and knees cleaning up the spilled oil on her floor. He was wiping furniture, the linoleum, and the carpet, everywhere there was oil, as she and her two children watched.

Now, all I can think is that the breaking plastic bag could have been the fault of a Publix front service clerk putting too many items in a bag, so the spillage on the linoleum floor *might* be Publix's fault. But the carpet? It sounded like the customer – or the customer's children – had tracked the oil onto the carpet. Yet, here was a Publix manager – I could picture him, in his long-sleeved white shirt and tie – on his hands and knees, cleaning the customer's carpet as well as the linoleum.

But I should kick myself. Thinking like a lawyer is a hard habit to break. And besides, Natalie's story wasn't finished.

After cleaning the oil, Mr. Singletary noticed that the intake on the air conditioner was clogged with dust. He proceeded to take out the a/c filter, clean it, and clean the vent.

Of course! I should have known!

The picture of Brian Singletary cleaning this customer's carpet – and then her a/c filter -- reminded me of Jim Rhodes cleaning out the customer's pizza-splattered oven. *It's not about fault*, I was supposed to understand. I could kick myself again for not remembering. *It's about making the customer happy.*

And Natalie *still* wasn't finished!

The next day, he had a professional carpet cleaning company go over to the woman's house and clean her carpet thoroughly. The woman was in awe. She absolutely couldn't believe that Publix or a store manager would do something like that for her.

As we've seen, strictly speaking, the Publix "guarantee" only guarantees a refund of the purchase price. But as I came to understand, Publix associates believe in the "afterthought" as well. *The sale is not complete until the meal is eaten and enjoyed.*

Publix meat coordinator Bakhos Zaiter tells of a time when he was the meat manager at a store back in the early 90's.

"A customer had purchased a bone-in leg of lamb for a special dinner," he says. "A short time before her guests were due to arrive, she realized that the lamb leg was a bone-in, and not a boneless, and that she did not have a knife, or the experience to carve it. The customer called the store in a panic. She explained her dilemma and I assured her that I'd help. I took down her address, went to her house, and carved the leg of lamb before her guests had arrived.

"The customer could not believe that someone would do that," says Bakhos. "She became my customer for life!"

One last story (for now). At Store 559, store manager Mike Chester was called to the deli to help a customer. The customer had ordered three platters, but had asked to have them ready on the wrong date. The customer was almost in tears because she had several people coming over in a couple of hours and did not know what to do. The mix-up was clearly her "fault," but that only made her more upset. Mike told her not to worry. They would prepare the platters and have them delivered to her house, to allow her to prepare for her guests.

"I knocked on her front door with platters in hand," says Mike. "She invited me in and asked if I would help her display them on the table. I could see that she was still in a panic because she was not ready for her guests. So I offered to stay and help."

Offered to stay and help? Mike understood that one of the things people remember for a long, long time, is being astonished.

"I know I made a lasting impression because every now and then, I'll have an associate tell me they bagged an order for a customer who told them about the day I washed her dishes and took out her trash."

Washed her dishes?

Took out her trash?

The sale isn't complete until the meal is eaten and enjoyed.

7.
A Little Better Place

*W*hat was Mr. George's answer to the secret of Publix's success? He once said: "The question I'm asked most frequently is, 'What's the secret?' 'How did you do it?'" His answer: "The most obvious answer, of course, is one word... people."

Having been in human resources all my adult life, I knew that Mr. George was right, that the secret to success is "people." Okay. But *what* is it about Publix associates that makes them so good at customer service? What do they do – and what *gets* them to do what they do – so that they're recognized, year after year, as among the best at it, anywhere?

One clue comes from another of Mr. George's sayings. It was one of those sayings that Publix decided long ago to put in handbooks and orientation materials, on banners at company functions and painted on hallway walls, inscribed on company pens and written in the margins of company calendars. Like the company slogan, 'Where Shopping is a Pleasure," and like the Publix Guarantee (and its all-important afterthought), this saying is repeated so often at Publix it would be impossible to avoid it.

Mr. George said it often.

Every one of today's Publix associates has seen it and heard it repeatedly:

"Publix will be a little better place, or not quite as good... because of you."

It's a simple thought. For a while, before I became a Publix associate, I brushed it off as simply stating the obvious. But beginning in 1992, as I came upon it day after day, it began to change for me. I finally decided it must contain a little yeast – because it *grew* on me.

It told me that as large as Publix had become, I, just one associate, was still important enough to make a difference.

It's a powerful concept.

Cathy DeVincent, now what Publix calls a "Retail Improvement Specialist" remembers her first days as a manager in the store, in 1997.

"I made a personal commitment to try to use customers' names whenever possible," she says. "This is something that I wasn't very good at, but I thought I'd at least give it a try. I kept a note card in my pocket and one of my first days there a gentleman came up to me and asked me if I was the new manager. I said yes I was and he introduced himself and his wife to me, shook my hand and said welcome. Well, I took my note pad out and jotted down their names, Howard and Ruth. I repeated the names over and over again. I swore to myself that the next time I saw them, I would use their names. Weeks went by and I didn't see them shopping. I was beginning to think it was a lost cause but, lo and behold, about six weeks later, they came shopping.

"I said, 'Howard, Ruth, where have you been? I thought you said you shopped here all the time?'

"Well, Howard stopped dead in his tracks, got very choked up, and replied, 'Cathy, I have been in business for seventy years and no one has ever bothered to remember my name.'

"I replied, 'Howard, if it was important enough for you to introduce yourself to me, then it was important to me to remember you.'

"I literally thought he was going to cry. But it made me realize how important the little things are in customer service."

In a business where the little things are important, it's critical to get every individual to realize the difference his or her individual effort can make.

Joe DeMartino was excited when he first got promoted to assistant common area manager in Boca Raton, but at the same time, nervous about the responsibility of having to make management decisions. One of those opportunities occurred a couple of weeks after his promotion, when he received a phone call from a customer we'll call Mr. H.

"He explained to me that he'd recently become immobile," says Joe. "It was due to an obesity disease he'd been battling. He asked if I could take a shopping list from him over the phone, gather his groceries, and then deliver them to his home, where he would pay me. Being newly promoted, *I wasn't sure if this was allowed,* but I figured it wouldn't hurt the store if I went the extra mile for a customer, so I told him I'd do it.

"I shopped for him. I rang it up on the register, bagged the groceries, and then delivered them to his home."

I only *suspect* that Joe DeMartino knows what a purple potato is, but I'm *certain* he's heard Mr. George's saying about Publix being a little better place "because of you."

Linda Owens, a housewares clerk in Columbus, Georgia, handles requests for special items.

"It always amazes me," she says, "the shock and surprise customers have when I call them regarding their request. I can't recall the number of times a customer has told me they never expected anything to come of their request – let alone get a phone call about it.

"One customer," says Linda, "wanted a specialty mustard that is a product of Oregon. She told me that she had recently moved to the Columbus area and had searched and searched for this mustard with no success. I told her I would see what I could do, and I would keep her informed of the progress. After two shopping trips I could not find the mustard. So I called her to let her know. She was very appreciative of my effort, but a little disappointed about not having this mustard. My next shopping day I actually found the mustard. When I called her again you would have thought I found the lost family dog! She was very happy. A *little extra effort* resulted in a very satisfied customer, and an associate being able to say, mission accomplished."

"Go the extra mile," says Atlanta Division vice president Bob Moore. "Our customers deserve it. The question I like to ask is, 'If we can do it, why not?'"

John Boatwright, a district manager, describes an occasion at Store 225 in Tallahassee. A customer approached the deli counter only to find other customers waiting ahead of her. The customer "rolled her eyes" with displeasure and left the deli area. An alert deli clerk, Alfred Greer, noticed her body language.

He could have ignored it. He could have figured it was something he couldn't help. But – just maybe — that saying of Mr. George's was in the back of his mind when he noticed the customer roll her eyes.

After Alfred finished serving the customers at the counter, he went looking for the customer and found her in the produce department. He apologized for not being able to wait on her right away, and told her that if she'd let him know what she wanted, *he would go get it while she continued shopping, and bring it to her.*

"The customer was overwhelmed," says John. "A *fantastic* job of customer service."

Publix associate Deonna Schaeffer used to handle the special requests for Store 683 in Fort Myers. She recalls an occasion when she got a request for Walden Farms salad dressings. She checked with several Publix warehouses. She even checked at some of Publix's competitors. But she couldn't find the brand. Regrettably, she had to call the customer to apologize for her lack of success.

Then, three weeks later, while on her last day of vacation in the Florida Keys, she stopped in the Publix there and happened to notice two bottles of Walden Farms brand salad dressing. Not content with just two bottles, she convinced her husband to stay over for an extra day (he loves to fish, she says) to await an additional shipment of the product. The next morning, she put three cases of the dressing on ice in a Styrofoam cooler and returned to Fort Myers with the salad dressing in her trunk!
"The customer was thrilled," she says.

In Nashville, after a customer thanked Wendy Jones for giving her a lift home from the store, Wendy realized how much such things could make a difference.
"It made me realize that although it's not every day that things like this happen, I am able to make an impact in much smaller ways," she said.

Two weeks before Christmas, Phyllis Sorey was working a grocery aisle in Coral Gables when she heard a little boy about five years old ask his grandmother, "How did all this stuff get into the store?"
Phyllis stopped what she was doing immediately. From a holiday display, she took down a Publix truck, pulled it out of its box, and gave the boy a demonstration.
"First," she said, "a big truck like this one parks behind the store. Then its doors open up…"
Phyllis opened the toy truck's doors. Then she grabbed some small cereal boxes and used them as an example of palletized product, demonstrating how the lift works.
When the boy still seemed confused, Phyllis took things a step further. She invited the boy and his grandmother into the back room. The boy's eyes opened in amazement when he saw the size of the back room. "Wow!" he said. "This is neat!"
Phyllis tried to convey how much lies behind the scenes at

Publix. For obvious reasons, customer letters don't rave about the service provided by Publix support people, but their coworkers often do. And the same commitment a person sees in Publix stores is evident there as well.

Grocery manager Devin Langston still raves about the day the normal grocery truck from the warehouse was stranded as a result of an accident on the interstate. The warehouse managed to re-select the entire order and dispatch it within two hours.

"I worked in the Jacksonville Grocery Warehouse previously" said Devin, "and to say that this accomplishment was nearly impossible is an understatement! What the warehouse associates dealt with, and obviously overcame, was unbelievable!"

Holly Lowe, another Distribution associate, remembers one November a few years ago. "I had only been with grocery shipping a few months. When I thought of the hustle and bustle of the holidays, I thought of shopping and cooking, never my job. Of course, I'd never worked for a retailer! I came in to work on the Saturday before Thanksgiving and discovered the stores had ordered exceptionally heavy. It was second shift. The phones were ringing off the hook. When the supervisors sat down to figure out how much each selector would have to throw, they kept shaking their heads and going back to the calculators. It wasn't looking good – if the math was correct, we'd be throwing cases until tomorrow!

"Bad news travels fast. Soon the selectors were grumbling and started slowing down. Morale was terrible.

"Then something amazing happened. The supervisors, Darryl Phillips and Jerry Loehman, both took an order and started throwing. Then Jason Robinson in Inventory took an order. Bill Pelham and Matt Edison didn't even work in Grocery, but when they stopped in and heard what was going on, they took an order. The selectors saw what was going on and attitudes changed immediately. The pace quickened and the mood in the warehouse was suddenly that of camaraderie and friendly competition.

"Needless to say, we did not have to work until the wee hours of the next day like we'd previously thought. We finished and were clocking out just after midnight."

Whether in the stores or at the distribution centers, when Publix people look around them, they see co-workers who are ready to make an extra effort.

Publix president Ed Crenshaw says customer service isn't just bagging groceries and carrying it to the car. "Great customer service is quality product. It's being able to fulfill a shopping list, and not making the customer go to another store because we didn't have what they needed. But it's also the friendliness, the way the customers are treated, the way they are recognized by the associate that's serving them, the way they're offered assistance. It's the way they are greeted when they come in, and it's certainly the way they're thanked when they leave the store."

"And you just don't get that anymore," he adds. "Customer service is almost a thing of the past. Customers have been so conditioned to receive poor service, that they really are amazed when they are provided with good service. I spend a lot of time talking to our people about how it's *easy* to "wow" a customer, because they have such low expectations of service. Any little thing that they can do, the customer appreciates."

Elena Layman was asked to go through the lost and found at Store 725 in Marietta, to dispose of any unclaimed items. But when she came across a pack of pictures of a boy playing soccer, she thought they might be something special for whoever had lost them. Having noticed that they'd been developed at Wolf Camera, she went to Wolf and conferred with the manager there until they determined who'd had the photographs developed. When Elena went back to her store, she placed a telephone call to the grandmother of the boy playing soccer. The customer was delighted, and amazed that someone would go to the trouble Elena had, to preserve a memory for her.

"I will be a customer for life," the customer said.

Because "the ordinary" eventually comes to be taken for granted, an essential part of *superior* customer service is the willingness to step up, to take the initiative, to do something *out of* the ordinary. People who ask themselves what the job *requires* are thinking like us lawyers – and they'll end up delivering the level of customer service that we lawyers are so well known for. Even people who show up for work thinking about doing again today the same thing they did yesterday aren't very likely to exceed the customer's expectations. To *delight* the customer, a person must be empowered to do the unexpected – and they must be alert to the opportunity.

What gets people to think that way?

Cashier Dorthea Vega in Columbus was surprised one day

recently when the manager in charge brought her a superior service token. Superior service tokens are one of the ways that Publix managers recognize exceptional performance by associates. Dorthea had just rung up groceries for a young couple with a child. The father had approached the assistant store manager, Richard Harper, and said he'd never been treated so special in any other grocery store. Dorthea didn't understand how what she'd done could be considered special. All she'd done was to be informative, she said -- and in this case, to pay attention to the couple's baby.

But what was routine to Dorthea was not routine to the customer. Simple as it may seem, people don't always understand what behaviors a company is looking for. (Some companies don't want to provide the kind of service Publix does.) The superior service token is one of Publix's ways of saying to Dorthea that her attention to the child *was* extraordinary, in the customer's experience – and was, therefore, the kind of behavior Publix values.

After Bonnie Mykytyn found the customer's ring in the recyclables bin (see Chapter 3), Mike Chester shared the customer's letter of thanks with her. "She responded," says Mike, "by saying that it wasn't anything she wouldn't have done for any other customer." But sharing the letter with her was a reminder. Even though such care and attention might not have seemed special to Bonnie, it was seen as very special by the customer.

Publix does its best to recognize such examples of individual initiative. When the Publix corporate office receives a compliment letter from a customer, it is shared with the associate who rendered the service, and it's copied to every manager in the "chain of command" between that associate and the president. The result is usually a flurry of thanks and recognition from *several* managers inside the company.

We all like recognition. Publix recognizes thousands of associates every year at a service awards program consisting of banquets and luncheons and presentations of service awards. It circulates customer compliment letters. It awards superior service tokens. All this drives home the message about what Publix values. Even more, it drives home the message that an individual *can* make a difference.

Visiting a store, a typical customer encounters more than a dozen associates. Working an eight hour day, a typical associate encounters several hundred customers. Therefore, at every store, every day, there are *thousands* of opportunities for a brief moment

43

of customer delight. Providing superior customer service is about taking advantage of those opportunities.

While the "ordinary" (how to operate a register, or how to bag groceries) can be put into training programs and "taught," the art of delighting customers with the *extra*ordinary is harder to set down in a book or a training tape. It comes from the moment. And from the spontaneous initiative of each individual. Like a new flavor, never tasted before, it has to be experienced. It has to be demonstrated. And when it happens, it ought to be celebrated.

I've seen Publix people, in the course of demonstrating initiative, make reference to Mr. George's simple saying, *'Publix will be a little better place, or not quite as good... because of you.'* That saying is an appeal to the heart of every associate, urging each to understand the power he or she has, and to be alert to opportunities to put that power to use. It is a seed of understanding, and it is a grant of empowerment. Repeated often, by managers and co-workers alike, it ends up moving people to extraordinary behavior.

Speaking of moving people...

In a number of stores where space is at a premium, Publix now has "people movers." Where lots aren't large enough for a normal supermarket and parking, it's sometimes good economics to build a two-story store. The basic problem at such locations is getting shopping carts up and down the stairs. So a few Publix stores have custom-designed escalators that take customers (and their loaded shopping carts) from the store (upstairs) to the parking garage (downstairs) – or vice versa. The Surfside and Miami Beach stores are two of them.

As store manager Joanne Mullery can attest, the "people movers" sometimes break down. And when they do, the store team faces special challenges.

"This occurred today," says Joanne's e-mail. "Our customer elevator and the people mover both went down at the same time. This meant the only way to get customers' groceries downstairs was to carry them by hand. Every department in the store, including managers, all pitched in carrying groceries and assisting elderly and handicapped customers up to the store and down with their groceries. It amazes our customers witnessing the team work on a normal day; [but today] the comments we received amazed us. 'You all look like you're having fun even when everything is going wrong.' To the bakery manager, David: 'Who's baking if you're taking my groceries out?'

"We have shuttled shopping carts via the freight elevator and we have carried customers down the stairs. The way our entire store jumps in and takes care of business makes me proud to be part of Store 73 and Publix."

Then, as if on cue, Joanne's e-mail closes, *"This is what Mr. George meant when he said, 'Publix will be a little better place, or not quite as good... because of you.'"*

8.
The Out of Stock

*T*he best way to handle out-of-stocks, of course, is to prevent them from happening in the first place. But when they do happen, there's an opportunity to delight the customer.

Cherie Dykers tells how she was looking for hamster food at the Lakeland Grove Park Publix. The store was out of stock. Store manager Tony Brooks asked her what she was looking for. When she told him, he personally checked the back room. When he found none there, Cherie told him she would go to another Publix and get some.

But Tony would have none of that. He asked her if she was going to be in the store for a little while longer. She said she was. Before Cherie had finished her shopping, Tony had bought some hamster food at another Publix and brought the product to her – personal delivery.

A customer in Hoover, Alabama, wanted two cases of Cavender's Greek seasoning for a church cook-out. Due to a misunderstanding with the vendor, only one case came in. The discrepancy wasn't caught until the customer came in to pick up the order the very day it was time to start marinating. Associate Rachel Horton got on the phone with other Publix stores in the area and was able to track down another case.

"When I told the customer we found a store that had some more seasoning for him, he thought he was going to have to go and get it himself. We told him he didn't have to worry; we would send someone out to get it for him. The customer said he was blown away that a grocery store gave this kind of service to anyone. Since then, this customer shops at our store every week."

This aspect of customer service at Publix is about convenience for the customer; but it's also more than that.

Jeff Sewell describes an occasion at Store 210 in Davie. He was a new manager, but the senior one on duty.

> It was a Sunday night. We closed at 10 p.m. At 10:50 p.m., we were about to leave when a 'more mature' lady was banging on the door as if she needed help. I went to the

door and asked how I could help her. She said please, I know you're closed, but I need some escarole lettuce to make soup. She explained she had a colicky grandchild at home that had been crying for hours, and needed to make this Italian remedy to try and calm the baby down. She looked as if she'd had a very difficult day, and was stressed out.

Our second daughter was still an infant. Since I knew what it's like to have an upset newborn, I went back to the produce department and found that we didn't have any escarole. I was thinking, what am I going to do -- this customer really needs my help!

I called a neighboring store to see if they had any left. Luckily, they were still there, but also about to leave. I convinced the manager on duty to wait for me to come and get it. I returned twenty minutes later and gave the customer the lettuce. I felt really good to have been able to relate to her situation and be able to help.

Stacy Isabelle was having a dinner party and she needed whole wheat lasagna noodles for one of her guests on a special diet. The Publix in Orlando where she shops didn't have the item in stock. Store manager Johnnie Hughes agreed to find out if they were available at any other Publix stores in the area. Ms. Isabelle returned home.

As it turns out, the other Publix stores didn't stock the noodles either. But at Mr. Hughes' instructions, the store located the noodles *at a local health food store*. About twenty minutes after Ms. Isabelle walked through her door, her telephone rang. It was Publix on the phone, wanting to know if it was okay to deliver them to her home.

"I'm in the marketing profession," said Ms. Isabelle. "And I appreciate the value of really good customer service. That's why I only shop at Publix."

If it seems surprising that a Publix associate would get an item for a customer from a health food store, consider the case of Ms. Barbara Murray of Canton, Georgia.

When a pumpkin pie mix she wanted was out of stock, Ms. Murray spoke to store manager Rick Harden. "I told him I would prefer to return the few items I had already put in my basket and do my shopping at Kroger this day instead, because I really needed this particular product.

"He offered to personally go to Kroger to get the product while I continued to shop...

"I stared at him briefly trying to comprehend what I had heard, and then agreed..."

"Every day is a different story," says Carlos Fonseca, an assistant store manager in Miami. "One day at Publix Store 204, I was approached by a customer who requested Peach and Cobblestone Nutrigrain bars. She said they were her daughter's favorite food. I asked the customer to give me a day or two to try to locate the product. I located the vendor (Keebler) and learned that the bars were discontinued and that Keebler no longer carried them. I checked with other Publix stores, and no one had any. I then decided to visit a competitor's store, and I was at last able to find it. *I bought all of the inventory.*"

Tom Keller of Norcross tells of the time a customer asked for a product Publix didn't carry. After checking with local competitors and finding they also didn't carry it, Tom ordered the item through Publix's special item request system – a process that would take about eight to ten weeks.

The customer was appreciative, but mentioned his "hope" that he and his wife had enough product on hand to last that long. So two weeks later, while on vacation with his family in Florida, Tom began checking competitors there, and on his third try, found the product at a Goodings supermarket in Orlando.

"I bought the few remaining packages that were on the shelf," says Tom. "When I told the customer how I'd found it, he joked and asked if my wife threatened to divorce me for taking her on a side trip during our vacation. I explained to him that my wife is also a long time Publix associate, so she understood."

These behaviors aren't isolated. They're repeated again and again. To understand them, it's helpful to recall what Ed Crenshaw said: "We never want the customer to leave the store unhappy." Or what former president Mark Hollis said: that his job was to "make the situation *feel* right" for the customer. This isn't just about keeping the customer from having a reason to go to a competitor's store. And it isn't even just about sparing the customer some inconvenience. It's about making sure the customer leaves the store *pleased* – whatever it takes – and looks forward to coming back.

Tom McLaughlin, vice president of the Lakeland Division, says he learned the true definition of customer service in 1975. A customer was unhappy after receiving a bad piece of meat from the store where Tom was then the assistant manager. There'd been an apology; the meat had been replaced; the customer had been given an apple pie; but she was still not satisfied. "For weeks," Tom recalls, "I'd been trying to satisfy her. I had gone above and beyond with kind words and even a potted plant."

Then Mr. George visited Tom's store. While there, the company's founder asked Tom if he'd satisfied the woman.

"'Mr. Jenkins,' Tom recalls saying, "we have done just about everything we could to make this customer happy, but I still don't believe she is satisfied.'

"He looked at me with those penetrating eyes and said, 'Well Mac, I guess you haven't done your job.'

"From that day on," says Tom, "I understood the meaning of customer service at Publix."

The focus, of course, is on making the customer happy. When this focus is reinforced often, it can become part of a person's blood. Publix retiree Bill Sneed told me a story that shows how deeply it had become a part of his.

It occurred years ago, when Bill was a store manager in Melbourne. Bill's customers – especially older ones – had been complaining it was too hard to open Publix milk in the gallon jugs. The new plastic caps were the problem. They were a new design, a big "improvement" that only Publix was using. One customer in particular was insistent about the problem. She simply couldn't get the stubborn plastic rings off the caps. Bill had inquired at the warehouse, only to be told that the caps were fine, that it was simply a matter of understanding the proper way to open them. Bill tried to show his customers the proper way, but even with practice, Bill found them difficult to open. He called the warehouse. Could anything be done about the problem? Find a new supplier? A new design? *Anything?*

The customer waited patiently for Bill to resolve her problem. But in the end, Bill had to tell her that the special plastic caps on the milk jugs were here to stay. The customer, in return, told Bill that she simply couldn't open the milk jugs. She would have to start shopping at Winn-Dixie – whose milk she *could* open.

Bill didn't want to lose the customer. So he asked her to give him one more chance. Bill asked her to ask especially for him the next time she was in the store. She agreed. The next time she came in, Bill went into the back room and got her several jugs of milk, with easy-to-open caps. The customer was delighted.

From that point on, Bill carried a "secret" inventory of *non-Publix* milk in his back room, just for the customers who expressed a problem with the new plastic caps.

Problem was, when people are happy, they like to talk about it.

Soon thereafter, Roy Raley, Bill's district manager, called Bill and said there was a problem. Roy was an old timer who'd started with Publix back in 1960. Roy said sternly that he had in his hands a copy of a letter that Bill's customer had sent to Joe Blanton, then president of Publix. The letter complained about the Publix milk caps, said Roy. But the letter also described how *helpful* Bill had been.

Now, usually, a manager feels good when the boss calls with a compliment from a customer. But Bill didn't feel good. He could hear the tone in Roy's voice. He cringed, knowing what was coming next.

"And the letter says how *resourceful* you've been, Bill – keeping an inventory of non-Publix milk in your back room!"

Bill was sure he was in hot water. Roy explained how wrong it was for Bill to be selling a competitor's milk, rather than doing whatever it took to sell Publix's milk. He told Bill the two of them needed to go out to the customer's house with some Publix milk, "no charge," and demonstrate to the lady the "proper" way to open the Publix milk.

"I've done all I can do," said Bill. "The blasted caps won't open."

"You haven't tried hard enough," said Roy. "I'll show you how to demonstrate these caps."

With that, Roy met Bill at the store. Taking several gallons of Publix milk with them, they drove out together to the customer's house. Bill says the place was like something out of *Better Homes and Gardens.* After getting pleasantries out of the way, Roy went to the kitchen sink and demonstrated how well the jugs were sealed. He held a gallon upside down over the sink and squeezed it, and everything was fine: the seal held perfectly. Then he said he would demonstrate how easy it was to open the caps. With that, he gave a quick tug on the little plastic ring, and it wouldn't open. He pulled again, harder, and still it wouldn't open. The third time, he gave it
50

such a hard tug, the jug slipped from his hands and a gallon of milk splattered all over the customer's beautiful kitchen floor. That afternoon, Roy and Bill cleaned up their mess and made their apologies.

A short time later, Publix changed the design of the plastic caps on its milk.

9.
Car Trouble

*T*he mission seems easy: shopping at Publix is supposed to be a pleasure, whatever it takes. Publix people really believe that the sale isn't complete until the meal is eaten and enjoyed, and are devoted to making that happen, too.

But the meal can't be eaten and enjoyed unless it gets home. And that means customers' cars need to be up and running. What happens when the customer is ready to go home, but the customer's car – after sitting for an hour under a hot summer sun or a balmy tropical moon – won't get up and go?

Judging from the number of stories received from associates and customers, I'll bet there's not a store at Publix that doesn't have several stories involving customers and their cars.

Countless associates have jump-started customers' cars and changed customers' flat tires. But while helping customers with car troubles may be commonplace to Publix associates, it's never commonplace to the stranded customer whose car has suddenly died. Those frustrated souls always have somewhere else they expected to be. Helping customers get their cars up and running again is an important part of making shopping a pleasure.

But if an associate spends more than a few weeks at Publix, dead batteries and flat tires won't be the only car problems he or she sees.

Store manager Manny Burrows and grocery clerk David Reid used a piece of baling wire as a fish hook, and fished the keys out of a car in which a customer had locked them in North Miami.

Michael Hardin of Spring Hill describes a customer who had dropped her car keys into the storm drain.

"She had parked by one of the large parking lot drains," says Michael. "The ones with the huge metal grates. When she got out of her vehicle, she dropped her keys, and to her dismay, she watched them disappear into the depths and darkness of the drain. The keys sank into the deep silt in the bottom.

"I told her I'd be back in five minutes. I went home and returned with my stepson's fishing pole. I carefully dragged the drain with a treble hook, side to side, back and forth, up and down.

The woman started sobbing hysterically. She proceeded to tell me her late husband's religious charms were on that key ring, and they were irreplaceable. Finally I felt something catch, and I carefully reeled in a messy set of car keys."

James Willis once responded to a distraught customer whose child had become entangled in the car's seat belt; with the customer's approval, James cut the seat belt in order to free the child.

Sometimes, things aren't as easy as solving the problem there in the parking lot. Walter Bishop went home, got his tools, removed a customer's battery and drove him to an auto parts store to replace it. In Lawrenceville, Brenda Sanders gave a woman a ride home after the keys got locked in the car.

"All the way to her house she kept going on and on that she just couldn't believe that I was doing this for her," says Brenda. "Ever since that day, she always looks for me to say hello when she shops. I always get to see the newest pictures of her twin grandchildren, and every once in a while, she will mention the day I did this small favor that meant so much to her."

A customer in Lakeland still tells about the time the effort to jump-start her car failed and she (and her groceries) were given a ride home.

"Twenty years later," says store manager Jason Macklin, "She's still shopping with Publix; and when she sees Wally, she still brings up that moment and thanks him."

And another posting on the Publix website:

On December 27, 2003, at approximately 8 p.m., I shopped in the store, went to my car and it failed to work.

I was with my young son and very worried. I spoke with a young man who was gathering carts out in the parking lot. He asked me to come into the store so that he could let his manager know I needed assistance. At this time, not only did the young man help, but the manager sent out several employees to assist me. One tried to give my car a jump, to no avail.

I went back into the store and the assistant manager called the deli manager – James T. Dodd. He proceeded to take me to the all night auto store to see if I could purchase a battery. They didn't have it.

Not only did Mr. Dodd proceed to take me and my son home, the next day, when I purchased the battery, he installed it in my car.

I would like to commend all your employees. Everyone was so helpful. I am a human resources manager. I understand the importance of great customer service. I can't say it enough – great job, great job.

April L. Floyd
Jonesboro, Georgia

Front service clerk Isaac Buteau works in Miami. One evening in November, 2003, he was walking home from work in the rain. He observed one of his store's older customers pulled off the side of the road with a flat tire. He stopped and changed the tire for her – in the rain – then refused her offer of a ten dollar tip, saying it was "just part of the service he learned at work."

Associate Jay Mattatall remembers a time his wife had run out of gas in a rough neighborhood of Palm Beach County. When he arrived to help, he couldn't get the car started, and it was getting dark. They put the hood up to get attention, but cars kept driving by – until a man and his young son stopped and asked what was wrong.

"I said I needed a jump. He was on his way to play basketball with his son and didn't have any jumper cables with him. But he went back to his house to get some. He returned fifteen minutes later, and we got the car started. I tried to give him some money for his trouble, and he wouldn't take it. I asked his name and what he did. Wouldn't you know, the Good Samaritan that stopped to help me was a Publix associate. His name is Alphonso Styles. I had a chance to see the Publix spirit in action!"

Scott Hirsch of Marietta remembers when he was a seventeen year old bagger, with Publix for less than a year.

"I had something happen to me that let me know the power every associate has," he writes. "Like every store, my store had its share of regular customers. And of course you always build relationships with the people you see over and over. That was the case with an elderly couple that I saw every Saturday. I enjoyed talking with them about their grandson, who was my age. But my story isn't about what happened while working, it was what happened the day I saw them at the gas station. I pulled in to get a tank of gas, and I saw my customers trying to change a flat tire. No one at the gas station was willing to help them – and boy, did they need it.

"I went over and changed their tire for them. I know I made a difference that day, and though I wasn't working at the time, to those two customers, I represented Publix."

Alright. You may be thinking it's natural for a retailer to help out a customer with car trouble. It's what *any* retailer would do. After all, customers can remember such an act of kindness for a very long time – so who wouldn't do as much?

If that's what you're thinking, then consider the case of Marlene Scalise, a part-time floral associate in Land O' Lakes.

"One day in October," writes Marlene, "I noticed a customer who seemed to be troubled. She was staring into the parking lot. This customer then began pacing back and forth over and over again. She had a cart overflowing with groceries. I approached her and asked if she needed help with anything, or if she was simply waiting for someone. She answered that she had locked her keys in her car. She also told me that her husband was walking home to get their spare set of keys. She explained that her husband is older, and has a heart condition, and she was terrified that he would run into problems on his way to the house.

"I asked, 'How far does he have to walk?'

"She told me about two miles each way.

"I suggested that we put her groceries in our floral cooler until he returned, so nothing would spoil or melt. After we got her groceries into the cooler, we carried on our conversation. But with every passing minute, she was growing more and more nervous.

"It was at this moment I went to my purse. I got my keys and held them out to her. 'Would you like to take my car to go pick up your husband and take him to go and get the keys?'

"She replied, 'Really? You would let me?!'

"I told her, 'Of course. Here are my keys and that is my car.' Needless to say, she ran all the way to my car and drove away.

"A little more than half an hour later, she returned to the store and came to the floral department. She had the assistant store manager with her. She was crying and thanked me over and over again.

"She then looked at me and asked, 'What would you have done if I didn't return with your car?'

"I jokingly answered, 'I would have kept your groceries.

They're probably worth more than my car.'

"We all shared a laugh together and I got her groceries out of the cooler. We loaded up her car and sent her on her way."

Loan a customer your car? *Extraordinary.*

Premier customer service is what made Publix what it is today, and company founder George W. Jenkins loved to deliver it himself.

"Mr. George" knew that being able to share a smile or laughter with customers helps to make shopping a pleasure.

Current CEO Charlie Jenkins, Jr., enjoys encouraging associates to carry on the legacy of premier customer service

10.
Relationships

Mr. George was often heard to say, "If you are going to be in the retail business, the number one thing is to please the customer." In the late 1970's commenting about the new scanning technology in the checkout aisle, he was asked whether increasing automation meant that Publix associates were any less important. His answer was an emphatic no.

"The personal contact with the customer will not be lessened any with all this automation," he said. "As a matter of fact, I believe it will be improved."

Mr. George is remembered as saying, "It's about treating customers and associates as individuals. As long as we take care of each other and the customer, and do right by each other, we'll make a little money along the way."

Jim Rhodes sums up what the founder taught him this way: "What I learned from Mr. George is that we're in the *relationship* business."

Michael Randall has been a customer of Publix for thirty years. He does his shopping on Sunday mornings. About a year ago, he began encountering a cashier named Karen Stillman. Mr. Randall didn't much care for Karen's attempts at conversation. According to Mr. Randall, Karen was "so bubbly and cheerful that she was actually a bit irritating. Sunday mornings I want to get in, do my shopping and get out."

But this long-time customer recently wrote to the company in praise of Karen, saying that her friendliness gradually grew on him until now, he'll wait in line at her register rather than go to an empty one.

In January of 2004, he and his wife Sherry had their new grandchild at home with them for the first time. They'd been talking about buying a baby carriage, and that Sunday morning, Mr. Randall noticed there were two carriages on sale at Publix. Mr. Randall describes himself as "the most ignorant baby carriage person in Tampa Bay," and he didn't want to make a decision alone. So he went to Karen's check out line, and stood behind another customer, waiting for a chance to talk to Karen.

When she'd finished the prior sale, he said to her, "Now you pay the price of all your good humor. You have to give an honest opinion to a customer." He explained he was undecided about the baby carriages.

Karen left the register and went with Mr. Randall to where the baby carriages were displayed. She inspected the baby carriage he had in mind, checked it out, moved it around, and discovered a few of the features, explaining them to him as she did so. She confirmed that the other carriage was for older children. At the end of her inspection, she told Mr. Randall that the carriage he'd asked about would meet her own tests, and she thought it was at a good price. After buying the carriage for $69, Mr. Randall got home to find out his wife had bought a similar model for a friend and paid almost a hundred dollars.

The customer's letter to Publix, complimenting Karen's service, shows a marked change from his initial irritation at her friendliness. The letter wasn't about the low price he'd paid. It was about Karen Stillman.

"Make no mistake," wrote Mr. Randall. "If she didn't like the baby carriage, she would have said so. We've become casual friends. The point is I knew I could trust her honesty and knew that whatever opinion she had on the carriage, it was far better and more informed than mine.

"In a sense, this is an 'old Publix' story," wrote Mr. Randall. "Know that you all are getting new, tough competition and that you have to react to changing times. But I hope you don't forget what I think are the keys to your success... courtesy and a basic respect for your customers. When I first started shopping regularly at Publix more than thirty years ago, these (and choice of products) separated your company from the others. For me, it still does.

"The baby carriage story isn't the only customer service story I can tell about Ms. Stillman. All she did that day was make me want to keep shopping at Publix. Had she knocked the stroller, she would have accomplished the same thing. In the end, you're not in the food distribution business, you're in the trust business. Ms. Stillman is great at what she does. You should know that."

Michael Randall
Wesley Chapel, Florida

"Our culture is in developing relationships," says Brek Williams, a store manager in Bradenton.

Jon Pastore, an office staff associate in Marietta, says, "I always make it a point to spend extra time making my customers feel we care about them as people."

Allen Norton started in Clearwater in 1955, when he was sixteen years old. He got transferred to several other Publix stores before becoming manager of his own store in Miami at the age of twenty-five. Allen describes how difficult it was to get out the front door of the store to go to lunch at his usual time of 1 p.m.

"The folks of my store's area, my customers, would always want to chat with me about different things. Now, *this is what I was there for…*" says Allen.

An interesting job description, I think; Allen saw his job as manager of a large store being to "chat" with his customers.

"*Buttttt*," he says, "I found it hard to get to lunch! So, on occasion, when I *really* had to get out of the store, I would go out the back door!"

Once I understood the importance of developing relationships, it was easier for me to appreciate the significance of Publix's "no-tipping" policy. That policy isn't just about making sure a customer doesn't feel obligated. It goes to the very nature of the relationship between associate and customer. Is a courtesy extended merely in order to get a tip? Or are courtesies extended, and smiles offered, because the customer is genuinely appreciated? Customers can tell the difference, and the prevalence of *genuine* appreciation is a fundamental part of forming relationships.

Consider, for example, Store 420 in New Port Richey. At that store, Jean Ann Helmholtz and Lil Roderick built a relationship with a mother and daughter. When they noticed the daughter not coming to the store, they asked the mother why her daughter hadn't been with her lately. The answer was that the daughter was having a problem pregnancy and confined to bed. Later, the daughter wrote a letter to the store, saying how special she felt that Jean and Lil had been asking about her.

At this same store, bakery clerk Gail Foley struck up a friendship with a customer who'd suffered a personal loss. And at the same store, a four year old boy always looks for Edna Mollohan, the store's meals clerk. (Once, he asked her if she'd be his friend forever.) Finally, when the deli clerks at Store 420 saw frequent customer Val come in without husband Tony, they asked her about him, only to learn he'd had a brain tumor. After some tears were shed, they pitched in and got a funny get well card and balloons for Val to bring home to Tony. They wrote on the card that they missed Tony's jokes. A month later, Tony and Val came in together to thank the associates for caring about them.

In Conyers, there's an ongoing relationship between the deli associates and customers Bob and Alice.

"They visit us at least five days a week to have lunch or dinner in the café," says store manager Mike Barr. "Last week, when it was Bob's birthday, the associates got with Alice and threw Bob a birthday party in the deli café. We had cake and ice cream and brought together Bob's children and close friends. Joy and fellowship was shared. I was very proud of our associates for creating relationships like this, that go far beyond just 'serving the customer.'"

Ryan Wright worked as a bagger in Lilburn when he met a couple he now affectionately calls "Mr. and Mrs. D."

"They took an immediate shine to me after hearing of my plans for college and my plans for a future career," says Ryan. "My friendship with them really took off after my promotion to the back office. Mr. D and I had numerous conversations about the progress of my education and he has told me several stories about his time spent as a U.S. Jumper. Unfortunately, Mrs. D suffered a severe stroke a few months ago, and has been in a local nursing home ever since. I felt awful about Mrs. D's medical troubles, and I felt even worse when I saw how hard Mr. D was taking the changes in his life. I visited Mrs. D several times and tried to help in every way that I could.

"One afternoon, I met Mr. D at the nursing home and assisted him in disconnecting the TV and carrying it to his car. Also, that afternoon, I spent some time with Mrs. D and a few of her closest friends. When the time came to depart, Mrs. D's friends stopped me in the parking lot of the nursing home and asked me what motivated me to continuously help this couple. My reply was that they were worth more to me than just friends. In fact, I sometimes see Mr. D as the grandfather I never had."

A sure sign that a relationship has formed is when a customer writes to express sadness that an associate is leaving. A letter from a customer in Oviedo raves about "the young adults at MY Publix – Marvin, Omar, Johnny and Jen." It says "Although I wish these young adults all the best, *I can't help feeling sorry to see them go* once they finish school."

A letter from a family in Naples raves about seafood specialist Paulette "P.J." Thompson. "We know she is leaving the area and will continue to work for Publix in north Florida. While we wish her well, *she will be sadly missed* by all of us down here."

Bette Shaia, an assistant store manager in Dacula, describes some regular customers at Store 569 who were always referred to as "Mr. and Mrs. B." "Mr. B became like a grandfather to many of our young people," says Bette. Then, Mr. B lost his wife.

"When we found out, everyone here at Store 569 wanted to be available somehow to let Mr. B know how much we cared for him and his wife. A group of about ten of us decided to make the trip out to Lithonia to attend the viewing and service for Mrs. B. When we arrived, Mr. B lit up like a 100 watt bulb. He immediately stopped talking to the person he was visiting and made an announcement to those nearby that 'his Publix family' was here. He hugged and greeted us all, and made sure we met all members of his family. Each time he was in our store after that, he would tell other customers about his Publix family and what we had done."

Such attachments, it's clear, still form a big part of customer relations at Publix.

How, then, do such attachments begin?

Andy Anderson is the owner of a small Harley Davidson repair shop in Deland. Andy and I were recently talking about customer service (discovering similarities between the service philosophies at Publix and at Andy's shop, which has only three employees) when Andy told me about his recent visit to Publix.

"I don't do the shopping at our house," says Andy. "My wife Sandy does. But this one day, I went with her – I don't remember why. We walked into the Publix in Deland. Right away, Sandy has to go to the bathroom. So she hands me her purse, and she heads off, leaving me standing there, with the purse in my hand."

To fully appreciate the picture, you should understand that Andy is a genuine biker. He owns about eight Harleys himself, including a classic 1948 model. With his beard, his long gray hair tied in a pony tail, and his black shirt, jeans and full-body tattoos, he makes for a striking picture even when he's not holding a purse in his hand.

"I'm standing there, waiting," says Andy, "and up walks this

Publix manager. I'd never seen him before, and I'm sure he'd never seen me. He looks me over head to toe, sizing me up. Then he says, 'Nice purse. It goes well with your shoes.'

"Now, he said this kind of challenging me, you know? I didn't know what he was thinking. I was ready to come right back at him. But before I could say anything else, he laughed and asked, 'You're Sandy Anderson's husband, aren't you?'

"I wasn't exactly wearing a name tag, you know. This guy had never seen me before. So I said, 'Yeah, I'm Sandy Anderson's husband. How did you know?'"

The point of Andy's story was made clear by the manager's answer.

"I recognized her purse," the manager replied.

Now, being alert enough, being *observant* enough to recognize a customer's purse, and to use that insight to let your customers know you care – *that's* customer intimacy. It made a big impression on Andy.

Back in 1989, Rick Llosa was on vacation when he met a couple from New Jersey, also on vacation, at Clearwater Beach. Learning that Rick worked at Publix, the woman mentioned she'd found a cleaning product at Publix – "Sno Bol" – that she could not find anywhere in New Jersey. When Rick got back to work after his vacation was over, he ordered a case of the product, paid for it himself, and shipped it to the couple in New Jersey. The two families have kept in touch and have been friends ever since.

It doesn't always take something that dramatic to get a relationship started. Bonnie Plesco, a customer from Brandon, wrote a letter of thanks after being helped in the deli by "a wonderfully happy woman."

"She wore a yellow veil on her head," wrote Ms. Plesco. She had been impressed by the associate's professional service and friendly attitude behind a busy deli counter, but that's not what motivated her to write. As Ms. Plesco was standing in the checkout line, the deli associate with the yellow veil was getting off her shift.

"She looked at me and acknowledged me, remembering me from the deli," wrote Ms. Plesco.

In this case, it was merely a look – some personal recognition from an associate no longer on duty – that so touched the customer, she mentioned it in a letter to the corporate office.

A relationship was begun that day.

The following e-mail was received from a ninety-year-old customer. It's about bakery associate Mary Murphy:

I want to applaud the efforts of Mary Murphy in the bakery. I am a ninety year old woman and I care for my husband who has Alzheimer's. My visits to the store are usually hurried, as I have to rely on others to stay with my husband while I shop. Mary has been so kind and thoughtful. She has called me to tell me if my favorite muffins are in. She has held a box or two for me upon my request. She is always ready with a smile and a kind word.

My experiences with Mary and Publix make me feel as though I have a friend to visit. With the loneliness of my husband's disease, I welcome that extra concern and effort. Thank you for allowing your staff to take an extra minute for folks like me. It really does make a difference.

A. H.
Cape Coral, Florida

Relationships usually begin with a single, unilateral gesture. It may be a simple hello, or remembering a customer's name. It may be a joke. It may be a bold act of kindness. Once that first action has set things in motion, it's amazing how the relationship can grow.

Recall from Chapter 7 how Joe DeMartino took the call from immobile "Mr. H." and agreed to the customer's request to delivery groceries to his home in Boca Raton?

"He was so appreciative of the service that he asked if he could do this again," says Joe. "I told him it would not be a problem. So every week, he called and I delivered. Over time, we formed a friendship. Every time I would see him, he would invite me in and we would talk and I would keep him company. Mr. H lived by himself and wasn't able to move a great deal, so he could never see any friends or neighbors. I believe Mr. H appreciated the service, but more importantly, he valued the friendship.

"I continued to do this for about a year until I was transferred to another store. Before I left, I informed Mr. H of the transfer but I brought along another associate with me (Paul) to introduce him to Mr. H, as Paul would be taking over the deliveries.

"I consider Mr. H, as well as other customers like him, an extra benefit of working for Publix as you get to see the rewards for going that extra step. I first knew Mr. H as a customer," says Joe, "but now he will forever be remembered as my friend."

In the case of customers with young children, there's often no better way to start a relationship than paying attention to the little ones. In fact, it's rare that a relationship can survive if young children are ignored. Amidst the piles of e-mails and letters and interview notes in front of me, there are scores that involve children. One customer posted the following e-mail at the Publix website:

Today I had the best experience. I arrived with my three year old. He was looking for a truck shopping cart, but none were available. There was an employee nearby, washing the windows and doors. He overheard my son's sad plea for the cart. So he went out to the parking lot and searched for a truck cart, but there were none available. We thanked him and began our shopping.

About fifteen minutes later (a third of the way into my shopping), this same young man came and found us in the store with a truck cart in tow. He then moved all of my groceries from the regular cart over to the truck cart. I need not tell you what this meant to my three year old boy, who loves to "drive the truck." I did want to tell you what it meant to me. What outstanding service!!! I was impressed when he looked in the lot. But to watch for one to become available, then to find me, was above and beyond.

My only regret was I didn't get his name. I just wanted to say thanks!!

Denise Hamilton,
Cummings, Georgia

Another customer wrote to compliment cashier Suna Evecan in Marietta:

I have been using your store since it opened. My children love to shop with me, not just because of the free cookies or the tasty samples in your deli, but also because, when I'm finished, Suna is always there with a smile and a great attitude. She knows both my daughters by name.

My husband laughs at the time my three year old sitting in the back of the cart saw Suna before he did. She almost climbed out of the cart and headed for Suna. I can tell you as a mother that it's a great bonus that I don't have to bribe her with candy to behave during shopping. I just have to promise that we will use Suna's line to check out.

When I see or hear a Publix commercial, I can't help but think of Suna. She works very hard. I have never seen her frown or look the least bit aggravated. I worked in retail for a while, and dealing with people full time and not only keeping a smile on one's face, but a good attitude, is a major accomplishment. She seems to really love people and what she does. She is a great asset to your store.

W. M.

Marietta, Georgia

This attention to children is common at every Publix store. In Lake Mary, there's a five year old girl named Alexis who always goes straight to see produce manager Scott McCarthy, to ask for a balloon or sing him a song. In fact, for Christmas, her mother made her *a doll* of Scott, so "she could play Publix." In Alpharetta, one customer wrote, "Jorge always takes time to pay special attention to my three year old son. My son so much enjoys this that he insists that we always shop at the store. With employees like Jorge, you don't need advertising!" In Miami, a customer raved about how Bruce Silva often has a stuffed animal or a Plato coloring book for her youngster. And in Tampa, a Publix customer was moved to send the company this letter about Penny Burland:

I have two young boys, ages two and five months, and I truly appreciate the extra attention and special service that Penny gives her customers. My older son scans the checkout lanes to find the aisle where she's working and refers to her as "*my Penny*." She manages to entertain toddler and baby while she assists me with unloading my groceries *onto* the conveyor belt. She sings to my children and efficiently gets us out the door with ease, consideration and kindness. *Penny seems to enjoy her job, deriving true satisfaction from helping others.* I will only shop at Publix and I prefer to shop when she is working.

Jennifer Hernandez

Tampa, Florida

According to Bill Slevin, store manager in Lake Mary, "you can usually tell where Linda Panarello, the meals clerk, is, by the laughter, and children's voices calling out to 'Miss Linda,' who gives great big hugs."

And at Store 695 in West Melbourne, which has a full-size

waterfall, front service clerk Andy Anderson buys rolls of pennies from the front office, which he keeps in his pocket, then hands out coins to young children so they can make wishes in the "Wishing Well."

From Nashville, Publix manager Lynn Gore writes:

> Dottie Holt (also known as Nana Dot) has truly wrapped her arms around the neighborhood and opened her heart to our customers and their families. Dottie came up with the idea to dress-up in a long dress, apron and bonnet, then read to all the children for an hour, twice a week. "*Story Time with Nana Dot*" was a real hit! The parents and children loved the stories, songs, games and surprises Nana Dot would share with them each week.
>
> Dottie is "Publix" to the core and is loving every minute of it! Customers are comforted by her when they let her know of loved ones passing or having surgery, and she buys them cards and roses. They feel welcome when she sincerely invites them over to her home for Thanksgiving dinner. They feel lucky when all she does is give a wink, smile or hug, and it changes the kind of day they're having."

As part of its commitment to keep stores new, Publix has one of the most aggressive remodeling programs in the industry. Its goal: that no store should go more than five years without a remodel. There are disruptions in the short term, as cases and signage and often whole walls and ceilings get torn out and replaced with new equipment and fixtures.

Of course, change can be unsettling. Customers rely on knowing just where to find a particular product; it can be disconcerting when your favorite product is suddenly in a different place than it's been for years. And even worse when it disappears altogether.

This was the problem after a remodel in Sarasota. Jerry Reed's store had just undergone a reconfiguration of its front end. Due to limited space, there was a casualty of the change: it was decided that the gumball machine had to go.

This change was a particular problem for one young customer, who wrote this:

Store Manager   1/9/04
Publix
Ringling shopping Center
Sarasota FL

Dear Sir,

Will you please put the gumball machines
back in the store because I used
to put 25¢ in them all the time
and I really liked them a lot.

Sincerely,
Paige Parker
age 8,

"We didn't think it would be a good decision to bring the gumball machines back into the store," says Jerry. "However, we didn't want to disappoint our young customer. So we decided to go to a toy store…"

A few days later, Paige Parker got the following reply:

WHERE SHOPPING IS A PLEASURE

Publix super markets, inc.

January 22, 2004

Paige Parker
2346 Gull Lane
Sarasota, Fl 34236

Dear Paige,

Thank you for taking the time to write and send me your letter.

I am truly sorry to hear that you are unhappy because we made the decision to remove the gum ball machines. We decided to remove the gumball machines due to the limited space in our store. We still have one left and it is currently in our associate break room. I would be happy to walk you to the break room whenever you are in the store, if it is okay with your parents.

Also, please accept this gum ball machine as a gift and let me know when you run out of gum balls and I'll be happy to send you more.

Sincerely,

Jerry Reed
Store Manager

In July of 2003, *Child* Magazine named Publix as one of the top ten "family friendly" supermarkets in the nation.

Recognition or not, it's evident to me that the focus on relationships remains as true today as it did seventy-five years ago. Publix associates still think of themselves as being "in the relationship business."

11.
Tough Nuts to Crack

*I*t's all well and good, you might say, to be friendly with a child. Or to come to the rescue when a customer's in need. Or even to be friendly and caring when a customer walks in the door smiling. But what about the customer who's angry at you, or at the world? How do you begin a relationship with someone when you've started out on their bad side? After all, some customers can be "tough nuts to crack."

In 1995, Store 184 had the reputation of being a tough store, catering to a more rural clientele. Word had it that these "country" folk did not like the idea of any changes.

Soon after Danny Lewis became the new store manager, his district manager, Rob Chapman, received a complaint from a customer. Rob arranged for both him and Danny to visit the customer. They sat for some time, says Rob, while "the customer unloaded everything that he did *not* like about Publix – and the world as a whole."

When he was finished, the man seemed pleased that they'd been to visit him. But he let Danny and Rob know that there was a group down at the local diner that was equally dissatisfied as he had been.

"If we were going to make any headway," he recommended, "we'd better get to know the rest of the 'gang'!" Danny and Rob agreed to go to the diner the following day for breakfast, to meet the group and hear their complaints.

The next morning, the two Publix managers sat and listened. The men were led by a very slender man in bib overalls named 'Bones.' But rather than pure bashing, as expected, the men spent much of the two hours praising the company. At the end, Danny shook hands with everyone, and then picked up the check for the whole group.

"The check and tip probably amounted to twenty-five dollars," says Rob, "but that act brought about a renewed loyalty to Publix and to their new manager. This simple act of respect for these men and their concerns turned one vocal customer into a 'breakfast club' – of which Danny became an honorary member. Even today, though Danny is working in another county, he still receives visits from the 'breakfast club' members and will, on occasion, go back to that little diner to swap stories, drink coffee, and listen to his 'old buddies.'"

Skipp Phipps once made a forty mile trip to deliver a wedding cake in Fort Pierce. Right before the reception, the groom's father looked at Skipp and asked, "What would happen if somebody did this?"

Skipp watched as the father proceeded to "ram his fist into the cake, punching a huge hole in it," according to Randy Strouse at Store 287 in Sebastian. Skipp then did a quick repair and cover-up job. The bride and groom didn't know about the damage until the groom's father told them after the wedding. After the honeymoon, they drove all the way to Sebastian to thank Skipp for his quick thinking and "saving their reception from humiliation."

When Don Ridgeway, store manager in Spartanburg, received a customer complaint via e-mail, he and district manager Dave Blankenship decided it didn't matter how far away the customer lived, they were going to visit her in person, apologize to her, and reassure her that they would work harder.

"This was about a 2 to 3 hour drive," says Don, '"but it was well worth it. She and her husband could not believe that we came all the way to her home just to apologize in person. Her name was Darlene and we took care of her like a queen..."

In December, 1998, Publix was named Progressive Grocer magazine's "Retailer of the Year." Publix President Ed Crenshaw told Progressive Grocer at that time, "Customer service is the way you treat people and how you interact with them. We develop this in our people right from the beginning, and by the time they get into management positions in the stores, good customer service is just a part of coming to work every day.

"It doesn't mean we don't get complaints or make mistakes," says Ed. "But when we do, we bend over backwards to make it right."

Here's an example of what Ed was talking about. A customer in Seminole bought some meat about ten o'clock one night; the meat leaked and got on the back seat of her car. She came back into the store, asking a manager for paper towels. But when the manager handed her the towels, the manager didn't express much concern about what the customer was trying to wipe up. (*Ouch!*) Very upset, the customer called the corporate office the next day to complain.

"We showed her the Publix spirit," said the store manager. "We went by her place of employment, and washed, waxed and detailed the inside of her car. This took approximately four hours. After that, she wrote a compliment letter, praising the outstanding service and attention she received."

Alan Thomas recalls being the on-duty manager at the Sawgrass store on the last busy day before a major holiday. It was almost closing time when he received an irate call from a gentleman who complained that when he'd gotten home, he'd discovered his turkey missing from his groceries. The store would be closed the next day for the holiday. But the customer, says Alan, "was very effective in screaming exactly how sorry we were going to be if we ruined his holiday."

The meat team located the kind of turkey the customer wanted from another store. The other store delivered the turkey to Alan, and Alan delivered it to the customer's home.

"I did the best I could to apologize," says Alan. "But he wasn't happy. He continued to scream about how incompetent we were. I left the scene feeling pretty badly.

"Ten days or so later," says Alan, "I got a call from the same customer. I braced myself for the onslaught. But he began by apologizing for how he had treated me.

"I said, 'No need to apologize, we should have taken better care of you.'

"He then said, 'No, you don't understand. Let me explain.' Earlier that day, he had noticed a terrible odor in his garage, and had started digging around. You guessed it – his turkey! Apparently, he was carrying in bags that holiday night, set it to one side to unlock the door, and the rest is history!"

Here, accepting responsibility (even when not at fault) likely made a lasting impression on the customer.

Tom Dean tells of an elderly lady he got to know when he was managing a store in Jacksonville:

"We knew her as Miss Alice," says Tom. "She used to get a ride to our store with a neighbor, but they'd had an argument, and the neighbor would no longer bring her.

"Miss Alice suffered from severe diabetes and spent her days either in a wheelchair or bedridden. She had not left her house in years. When associates delivered groceries, Miss Alice would always complain about her situation. No matter how nice and understanding our associates were, she was often mean-spirited to them. On one occasion, a frozen food clerk named James was given the delivery task. It was nearly Easter, and Miss Alice was in a particularly bad mood. She told James that no one cared about her; that she could not afford any Easter lilies; that if her family cared about her, they would bring some by, but she knew they wouldn't. James did his best to cheer her up, but with no success.

"When James returned to the store, he told me about his visit with Alice, and suggested that perhaps, if we had an abundance of lilies that might not be sell-through, we could take some to her.

"On the Friday before Easter, it was apparent that we would have some extra lilies. James picked out a few pretty ones and took them to Miss Alice's house. When he arrived, Miss Alice told him she hadn't ordered anything. James told her that someone had called the store and arranged to have these lilies delivered. Miss Alice accepted them without comment, and James arranged them in her room.

"When James returned to the store, I asked him how it went. He explained that Miss Alice didn't seem to care about the lilies. She hadn't even said 'Thank you.'

"The week after Easter, I was called to the office. There I saw Alice, with her neighbor. With tears in her eyes, Alice told me that she knew the flowers were from the store and it was the best gift she had received in years. That act of kindness had restored her faith, she said, and had made her decide to start living again. We would not have to deliver her groceries any more – she had patched things up with her neighbor and she would be coming to the store to see us every week.

"It's amazing what a simple act of kindness can do," says Tom.

Turning a tough customer into a fan can be difficult. Some of them seem impossible. No one knows this better than Helen Hartley, a demonstrator in Jacksonville. At an all-store meeting she attended one Saturday morning, associates were asked to "step up" on customer awareness and remember to greet customers they encountered. That afternoon, when Helen came into work, as she walked down the aisle on her way to her station in the back of the store, she passed a gentleman standing near the soap aisle.

"Good afternoon," she said, practicing her customer awareness. But she got no answer.

So she stopped and turned back to the gentleman, and said, "Sir, is everything okay?"

Again, there was no reply.

As I've said, some customers are very, very tough. Helen realized it might be a long time before she formed any kind of relationship with this particular gentleman. For he was no ordinary shopper. Overcoming her embarrassment, Helen approached her manager, Jack Felts, and told him about her attempt to practice good customer relations with the *cardboard mannequin* of a race car driver promoting Tide.

Tough customer, indeed!

In the case of customers with young children, there's often no better way to start a relationship than paying attention to the little ones.

12.
Special Occasions

*O*nce they're established, keeping relationships nourished and healthy requires an ongoing commitment. Relationships have to be respected. For example, being a parent means you're expected to do something for your children on their birthdays. Being a spouse means you're supposed to remember your wedding anniversary. If a company wants to be in the "relationship" business, it must be sensitive to customer feelings on those special occasions.

A customer of Store 443 in Winter Haven, Florida, telephoned Craig Magedanz, the bakery manager there, a bit timidly. She had a request that she knew was a bit unusual. The caller was a regular Publix customer, she said. But her sister was not. For their parents' 40th wedding anniversary, her sister had bought a cake at a competitor.

When they went to pick up the cake at the competitor, they were dissatisfied with the decoration. They asked the competitor if the cake could be redecorated. No, it could not, was the answer they got. But being somewhat pinched for time, they took the cake anyway.

Now the customer was calling Craig at Publix. Was there any way that *Publix* would be willing to redecorate the competitor's cake? Of course, was the answer. Sharon Boggan, decorator, scraped the cake and redecorated it for them. Both sisters were delighted.

Raymond Graham at Store 320 took matters up a notch when he got a call from a dutiful daughter. Here's how the customer described what happened:

> Raymond Graham of the meat department made father's day really special. I no longer live in Jacksonville with my dad, but I wanted to send him a nice cut of meat. Omaha Steaks wouldn't ship it in time for Father's Day. So I called up my dad's Publix to see if they had the chateaubriand I wanted at Omaha Steaks. Mr. Graham assured me he had it, and his was better than Omaha Steaks. And what's more,

he was willing to deliver it to my dad personally. And he did it – *dressed in a suit and tie, with the meat beautifully presented on a tray with balloons*!

Dad was totally blown away, so I am covered in glory. Mr. Graham refused to charge me for delivery. I just wanted to make sure you knew what a fine store and what an excellent man you have working for you there.

Ana Canales
Pensacola, Florida

Back when George McKinney was a store manager, one of his customers came through the front door with a decorated birthday cake in her shopping cart. She was crying uncontrollably. Makeup was streaming down her face.

He took her to the employee lounge, where he got her calmed down enough that she could explain what was wrong: the cake was for her ten-year-old granddaughter. And it had to be perfect, because the girl was dying of leukemia. This would be her last birthday cake. While the cake was beautifully decorated, it had been made of lemon cake, rather than her granddaughter's favorite – pound cake – as she'd ordered.

7:30 was birthday party time. It was already nearly 6 p.m.

"I assured her we would make this right," says George. "And that we'd deliver it to her home before 7:30 p.m."

But when George got to the in-store bakery, he found all the decorators gone.

"I couldn't waste time trying to get in touch with them," recalls George. "We had two part-time counter clerks, and one clean-up clerk, on duty – and I didn't know if we even made birthday cakes out of pound cake or not. But I was about to try. We did sell pound cake, delivered to us from the bakery plant. But we had only six cakes, and I needed eight to make a cake the same size as the one the customer had returned. So I sent one of my stock clerks to Store 263 to get two more. While he was gone, the counter clerk and I shaved the crust from the pound cakes and smoothed them together to make a larger cake, adding the other two when the stock clerk returned.

"I had never decorated a cake," says George, "and neither had the clerk that was helping me. But I *had* worked with mortar and bricks. We decided I would try to ice the cake, and she would try to decorate it. I remember thinking, as I iced the cake, that it was like laying mortar – and sure enough, it turned out smooth and even. While the young lady was putting on the trim and decorations, I found a cashier who could write like an artist, and got her to finish the cake with writing.

"This was a group that did not know how to create a cake, but we looked at our special cake with pride. I wish that we'd had time for pictures. I jumped in my truck and delivered the cake to our customer's home with ten minutes to spare. I thought that this family was going to hug me to death. They were very pleased with our cake. (Grandmother was still crying.) I went back to the store and thanked the associates who had helped me save this special occasion for this family.

"About four weeks later, this same customer was back in the store, asking for me. She was crying again – this time, because she had lost her granddaughter. We cried some more. Until this day, I've never told this story to anyone before," says George.

Finally, George adds one more thought:

"We were just doing our jobs," he says.

The thing about special occasions is that no matter how "routine" they may seem to the Publix associate, they are always "special" to the customer, and so whatever happens on them – good or bad – is apt to be remembered for a long time. A customer wrote this note "to whom it may concern" at the corporate offices:

> On 13 July, 2003, for only the second time in seven years, all seven of my parents' grandchildren would be in the same place at the same time. To commemorate this wonderful occasion, I ordered a cake from the bakery at my neighborhood Publix. I requested that each child's name be listed, and asked whether it would be possible to decorate the cake with six little plastic girls and one little plastic boy, each representing one of the grandchildren.
>
> On 12 July, I received a phone call from Julie at the Publix bakery (Store 414). She wanted to confirm which of the seven children was the boy, and she asked me to describe each child's hair color. I assumed she had a choice of plastic characters and wanted to match them to each child as closely as possible. I was touched and delighted... but I was wrong.
>
> You cannot imagine how thrilled each of the children were (not to mention the adults), when they saw that each of

them had been "painted" in frosting on the cake. It was magnificent. Julie's thoughtfulness and talent could not be more appreciated. *Her special contribution to our special day will always be remembered.*

S.D.

Naples, Florida

If there's any occasion that's special for a feeling of family and relationship, it's wedding day. And like the peals of wedding bells, the memories of such days linger on and on. How long people remember wedding days is something anyone interested in relationships does well to remember.

On a busy Saturday afternoon the Publix bakery in Macon got a call from a father with a problem. The wedding cake they'd gotten from a caterer was ruined, and the ceremony was about to begin. The florist for the wedding had suggested that Publix might be able to help. Carrie Tompkins, bakery manager, prepared a beautiful cake in less than an hour.

"I delivered the cake just as the ceremony was starting," says Dennis Curry, store manager. "The father explained that the cake had collapsed, and when they called the caterer, they were told that once a cake is delivered, they have no more responsibility for the cake. The cake we delivered was great, and they were extremely grateful. They immediately got caught up in the wedding ceremonies and I just left out the back door."

I'd have been right there, congratulating the caterer for understanding the limits of their legal obligation. Once the cake was delivered, they had no more responsibility for the cake. Absolutely right! But by doing something so clearly *not* required, Dennis and Carrie proved again what Publix does that generates raving fans.

"A few years back," says Tom Flaherty, a store manager in West Palm Beach, "our cake decorator Kim Trotman was called by her neighbor (a Winn-Dixie employee) in distress. Winn-Dixie had delivered her wedding cake and set it up. Later it had collapsed. Winn-Dixie wouldn't come out to fix it, because it was alright before they left. Kim came to her rescue with her Publix uniform on, and fixed the cake better than it was before. The word got out to all attending what had happened. And her neighbor shortly left her employment at Winn-Dixie and started at Publix."

Making weddings special isn't only the business of the bakery. In Tallahassee, a customer called assistant produce manager Craig Leckey in a panic. The customer's wedding was early the next day. The florist had completely ruined the flowers, and this customer needed eleven dozen different colored roses for the arrangements. To make things worse, it was the Friday before a holiday, so none of the local florists had any to spare. So Craig called the supplier that he orders flowers from, and drove *several hours* that same afternoon – from Tallahassee to the junction of Interstates 10 and 75 – where he had a "roadside rendezvous" with the supplier. He was able to get the roses the bride needed. Then, his floral specialist Judy DuBose came back to work on Friday evening to make the arrangements.

What is the impact on the customer in such situations? Consider what one customer wrote about her near-disaster:

This could only happen in a small town that has a great Publix store.

It was 3:30 in the afternoon on January 9th, 2004. My daughter's wedding would be at 7:00 that night and we were looking forward to a beautiful wedding -- and having the rare occasion of having all our friends and family at one place at the same time. Everything was wonderful. That is, until I received a phone call saying that the cake had not yet arrived at the church and the wedding guild was getting concerned. I contacted the person who was supposed to be taking care of it. To my utter dismay, she had marked her calendar wrong and had not even started the cake!

I immediately thought of Publix. I knew Mr. Jones, the manager of the Plant City store, and tried to contact him personally at his home. He wasn't home so I went to the store. By that time, it was 4:00 p.m. I asked for the assistant manager, Mr. Hancock, and explained my situation to him. Believe me, I almost 'lost it' at that time. My daughter's wedding was in three hours and I was expecting three hundred people to come to the reception. I asked him to help me and we went straight to the bakery. After a few moments of consulting Charlie Bailey, the bakery manager, they were able to tell me that they thought they could do it. Mr. Bailey explained that his decorator was scheduled to come to work soon and if he prepared the cakes for her, he thought she would be able to finish it.

That fabulous decorator is Vonda Maxwell. They planned to put several layered tiers together for the bride's cake. I was delighted when Mr. Bailey offered a chocolate sheet cake for the groom's cake. I left the store feeling relief and was feeling confident that the job was going to be done. Not only did they construct and decorate the cakes, but they delivered them on time as well. The cakes were beautifully decorated and the guests commented on how delicious they were.

I can't wait for the wedding pictures to arrive. I want to have a permanent reminder of how Publix employees went the extra mile for someone they didn't even know. I will never forget how they came to my rescue.

Deborah Schreffler
Plant City, Florida

Genuine relationships mean people really caring about people. Recognizing this, it isn't about the sale of a cake, but about helping someone out with a special life memory that will last for years.

Customers remember these occasions. If they sense that the sales clerk is interested in how much longer it is until quitting time, their experience will be negative. If they sense the sales clerk is interested in making a sale, they'll be satisfied, but unimpressed. But if they sense that a sales clerk is genuinely interested in their happiness – and willing to go out of the way to achieve it – the gesture that makes them feel that way is a gesture that few of us can ignore. We'll remember it for years, and possibly for a lifetime. More importantly, we'll want to respond in kind. We'll want to return the kindness. And we'll want to go back for more.

13.
The Holiday Spirit

F or many of us, holidays are a time to forget entirely about "the job." How many workplaces have become ghost-towns as people leave early on the last workday before Thanksgiving, or the day before the Fourth of July? At most retailers, the holidays – and the days leading up to them – are extremely busy times. This is certainly true in the super market industry. As the store gets hectic, the stress on everyone's nerves increases. The ability to give service with a smile can break and explode into the opposite. A real test of a company's customer service strength is its performance at holiday time.

If the company wants to sustain *relationships* with its customers, it needs to do more than just avoid stress-induced breakdowns at holiday time. It needs to *rev up*. It needs to *participate in* the holiday spirit.

In January, 2004, a customer posted this comment on the Publix web site:

> It was Christmas Eve day. The parking lot was jammed. I braced for what is typical fare in a tourist destination area – rude people who are locusts when they hit the staples like bread and milk – loud, boisterous, dangerous with carts, and operating with the firm belief that their time is more valuable than everyone else's. All this comes with exclamation points on special days like Christmas Eve. The things "day-mares" are made of.
>
> The experience inside the store stunned me, and I think a minimum of 90% of the credit goes to the team on duty.
>
> There was not a single item on any shelf that was not plentiful. The re-stock team was in every aisle. Everyone I said hi to smiled (although how is beyond me). No line was longer than every-day stuff at the check-out. Almost every register was open, they all had packers, and people went out with full baskets at about the same pace new people came in.
>
> Customers were *polite* – outright *courteous* to each other.

They said "excuse me" a lot, and even helped one another find things on the shelves, let them go ahead in line if they just had a few items... incredible!

I have not a shred of doubt: all that happened because the people working today set the tone. Friendly, not a trace of irritation or impatience, on top of everything and anticipating what people would want and need... I can't say enough good things.

My request: I hope you will pass my thanks and high-fives on to the manager and the team.

With warm wishes for happy holidays.

P.H.
Fort Myers, Florida

In Charleston, cashier James West has come to be known as "the candy man." For about two weeks leading up to holidays such as Easter, Halloween, Christmas, and Valentine's Day, James buys candy and keeps a basket of it out for the children who come through his check-out lane. He's been doing that – at his own expense – for three years.

"Eventually," says James, "even big kids started looking forward to seeing me with my candy basket."

On Christmas Eve, 2003, Jim Ammons visited the store in Loganville, looking for a gallon of eggnog. It was around one o'clock in the afternoon. Unfortunately, there was no eggnog left. Mr. Ammons was told that a shipment would be in around two p.m., but he replied that he really didn't want to wait around until then. Carter Vaverek, store manager, was standing nearby and overheard the conversation. He asked where Mr. Ammons lived, and said that he'd be happy to deliver the eggnog that evening on his way home. When Mr. Ammons protested that that wouldn't be necessary, Carter replied that no one should be without their eggnog on Christmas eve!

Carter delivered the eggnog as promised that evening at about 5:30. Mr. Ammons wrote to the company: "Only at Publix would this have happened. Keep up the good work, continue to hire and train employees like Mr. Vaverek, and we will surely continue to come."

At Store 53 in Hollywood, it was just a couple of hours away from the Jewish New Year when a call came in from an elderly customer who was distressed to realize she had no challah bread with which to celebrate the new year. She'd had challah bread for every new year that she could remember, she said, and didn't know what she was going to do, as she was not able to leave her house. Bakery Manager Mike DeFrancisco lives north of the store, and the customer lived several miles south, but Mike delivered the customer her challah bread when he got off work for the day.

And consider the following letter:

I would like to let you know that I am a single parent unable to afford much [and] I thought your prices were too high for me. On December 22, 2003, I found out that was not true. I visited your Store 881 in Winter Garden, Florida, because I received a gift certificate. Upon shopping there, I found out that your prices are very competitive. And, I had the best experience that will stay with me forever.

A cashier, Nancy Perfetto, checked us out. When we got our total, I was short some change. She took out of her own wallet the change we needed and said, 'Have a very merry Christmas.' She really made my holiday and showed my children what I have been teaching them all of their lives. Nancy did not have to do what she did for us, but it was the nicest thing I have seen anyone do in a long time. Because of her, I will continue to shop at Publix only, because I know they care.

Angela Everd,
Winter Garden, Florida

Cathy Tibbetts is an associate in Publix's human resources department. Cathy's husband, Dennis, is from Michigan. "He hears me talk about how special Publix treats its customers all the time," she says, "but he's now a solid believer in what I've been saying."

Cathy explains: "I began to make pies for our Thanksgiving dinner Wednesday night about 9:15 p.m. While mixing the ingredients I realized my bottle of vanilla was empty. Well it just isn't Thanksgiving at our house without pecan pie. So I thought nothing of rushing my husband out of the house to get some vanilla. When he pulled up to the store, there were a few associates still talking in the parking lot. They confirmed that the store had already closed. But when Dennis explained his need for the bottle of vanilla, one of them – John Wentworth – went inside the store and got a bottle of vanilla off the shelf for him!"

Consider how two managers in Kissimmee made this customer's holidays:

> My boyfriend Peter and I want to extend our sincere appreciation and thanks to two of your managers, Russell Fountain and Ted Reese.
>
> Peter and I wouldn't be together for Christmas. A weekend trip to Orlando in December was all we had to make the season special for us. Peter and I stopped by Publix Store 570 looking for a Christmas tree and some other necessities that would make our hotel room a cozy getaway for the holidays.
>
> When we arrived at the store, there was only one tree left. The bottom half was in pretty poor shape. It stood about six feet – too tall for our hotel room. Mr. Fountain and Mr. Reese immediately went to work. They cut the tree down to suit us (and the room), and they gave us the tree for free. Then they showed us where the tree stands were, the champagne, some snacks, and to our surprise, some firewood! (Yes, our hotel room had a fireplace.)
>
> To make a long story short, this was my first real Christmas tree and I couldn't have been more excited. We were extremely impressed with the service these two Publix employees extended to us. Peter and I returned to our hotel where we put up our tree and started a fire in the fireplace. Although the tree had only one small strand of lights on it and no other decorations, it was exactly what Peter and I wanted for this romantic evening away. Again, my sincere thanks to both Mr. Fountain and Mr. Reese for making us feel at home in their store.

Karren Branch has worked for Publix since 1968 – currently, in the Deerfield Distribution Center's maintenance department. She started working for Publix in one of the Miami Division stores, where she worked for 12 years.

"You know," she says, "you wait on customers for years, and you never realize that some are completely alone in this world, and that they'd like to know that someone cares. I remember an incident that has stayed with me for 36 years. I do not remember the year or the lady's name but I will never forget that Christmas.

"Around the holiday I was walking down one of the aisles when I noticed this very elderly lady crying. I asked her what was wrong and she cried and said, 'Today is my birthday, I am 82 years old and nobody cares.' I told her that I cared and that I looked forward to seeing her in the store again soon.

"When I got home that day, I told my husband about the incident and I asked him if we could invite her for Christmas dinner. We decided that if she came into the store again that we would invite her. Well she came in and I invited her to our home for Christmas. She was thrilled. I went shopping and bought her a few gifts. We picked her up from her home and returned her that night. She had a wonderful time. About three months later I read in the paper that she died.

"To me, even after all these years, I still believe that this is what Publix is all about: letting our customers know that we care."

What's done for someone on a holiday can do amazing things for people's spirits, and therefore, for relationships. Rather than succumbing to holiday stress, caring at Publix seems to rise at holiday time.

Donnie Poole in Northport, Alabama, went to some lengths putting together holiday baskets that a customer's church distributed to the needy.

"The holidays are a glorious time of the year," says Donnie. "Mostly everyone tries to be a little nicer to everyone else. Simple human kindness can go a very long way sometimes. You can put a smile on a face that was absent of one, or you can warm a cold heart with a tiny spark of kindness."

He describes how the customer thanked him for his help, and told him of the joy the holiday baskets brought to those who received them.

"I was able to have a hand in helping out my fellow man during the holiday season," says Donnie. "After all, isn't that what the holidays are all about?"

Finally, here's a letter written about a customer's experience when she checked out through Lynda Pritchard's express lane on Christmas Eve:

December 27, 2003

Dear Sir or Ma'am,

I wanted to take this opportunity to tell you a quick story before it slipped my mind. I was in your store on Christmas Eve. It was around noon, and I was standing in your express line – it was definitely *not* moving expressly, but that was fine with me. A young girl walked up and took over the register. Noticing the line was looped around the corner, she smiled and simply said, "—and you thought this was express!"

Some grinned, and most continued to stand there. She moved quickly and she was so friendly. When it seemed the line was not moving at all, she simply stated, "Everybody, now..." and began singing Jingle Bells! Most of the people in this line were elderly, and the men joined right in, believe it or not. This is just the beginning of the story, for little did that young girl know what she had done for me that day.

I lost my husband about two months ago, and we had been together for 58 years. I was standing in that line picking up a few things to get me through. I was in no mood for the holiday spirit. When that young girl had everyone sing, she changed my mood, for it was at that moment, seeing those men sing, with huge grins on their faces, it reminded me so much of my beloved Frank and how much he loved life until the end. I realized at that moment that I was to carry the joy of his memory in my heart always. When I finally reached the register and it was my turn, I simply took Lynda's hand and said thank you. She smiled real big and looked like she had no idea what I was talking about. Then, she simply said, 'Have a merry Christmas.'

I wanted her to know that, because of her, I did. And I intend to carry the joy of that moment, surrounded by strangers, and the huge heart of one young girl with me throughout the rest of my time on earth.

Tell her thank you and God bless her also.

Mrs. F. D.
Melbourne, Florida

14.
Any Day Will Do

*A*s important as birthdays, weddings and holidays are, relationships must be sustained day in and day out, whenever the opportunity arises. And as we've already seen, this means associates who are both empowered and alert. Because finding the opportunities on "ordinary" days is harder than finding them on special occasions.

An e-mail from one customer describes her mother's experience at a Publix store in Atlanta. The customer's mother went to Publix to pick up some goodies for football watching. After leaving the store, she turned around and went back in again – not because she'd forgotten something, but because she simply *had* to get the names of the cashier and front-service clerk who'd checked her out. She got the names – the cashier was Arturo, and the front service clerk was Angel – and (since she was only here on a visit) she made sure her daughter passed on her compliments. According to the customer, her mother said *she'd never been treated so well at a grocery store.*

What was all the fuss about?

Not for any anything spectacular. It was because Arturo had been "sweet," and both associates had been "kind."

No home deliveries. No found children. No free products. Just "sweet" and "kind."

What is it about "sweetness" and "kindness" that can cause a customer to take the time to write to a company? Sadly for the world we live in, the fact is that if it's genuine, it has become unusual. Unexpected. *Extra*ordinary. But happily for Publix, it's really not all *that* difficult to do, even on the ordinary days. You just have to be alert, and look for the opportunities.

Customer Rebecca Mitchell left her purse in a shopping cart in the parking lot of a store in Fort Myers. Realizing what she'd done, she returned to the store to look for it. First one associate, then another, joined in the search. When department manager Alex Blanco learned of the situation, he assigned associates to check the registers, the customer service area, the bathrooms, and the garbage cans out front. Eventually, the purse was recovered.

"But the real story here," Ms. Mitchell wrote to the company, "is how quickly, professionally, and compassionately *all* the employees reacted. I could have been a relative, they were so helpful. Every time I go back to the store, I am greeted with a special hello from my comrades in the search, and Mr. Blanco always asks me how I am doing. I haven't felt this kind of personal attention in any grocery store. Freshness, cleanliness, and prices are always important, but if employees are rude, sullen, or take out their bad days on you, you'll just go down the street to Albertson's.

"I think you do the most important thing in your stores. You make me feel like you *want* to assist me, and not that you are paid to."

Now, that gets to the heart of the matter. What Ms. Mitchell expresses so well is evident in many customer letters.

"Anyone can learn about the supermarket business," wrote customer Duke Schneider in praise of associate Dennis Tucker. "But it takes special talent to be genuine and sincerely helpful to customers. You can't fake friendly and sincere customer service. If you have it, it shines through like a beacon of light. If you don't, it won't even equal the flicker of a candle."

District manager John Westall sent me an insightful story:

When Ms. V couldn't find a particular type of bread in the bakery, she asked a clerk about it. The clerk said the bread would be available the following day. The following day, when the bread still wasn't available, Ms. V became upset.

Going to customer service, she found common area manager Marysia McFann. As it turns out, the customer's mother was under the care of Hospice, dying of lung cancer. There were very few things that brought her pleasure any more, and this bread was one of them.

Marysia called Suzy Perron, the bakery manager, and after consulting with her, Marysia told Ms. V a loaf would be delivered to her house in a few hours. A few hours later, office staff Tom Cruse arrived at Ms. V's door with the bread, Marysia's apologies, *and a pot of flowers.*

"I was touched," said Ms. V. "I am telling everyone I know about the incident. Thank you from the bottom of my heart."

"Sometimes," says store manager Larry Hill, "customer service is about listening to what the customer is really trying to tell you. According to Marysia, it wasn't the inconvenience – Ms. V did not want to disappoint her mother."

Listening to the customer. Understanding what the customer really wants, or is really pleased by, or is really upset about. Taking the time to really understand what's on the customer's mind.

In Lake Park, when a customer reported that her eight year old child was missing, the store team searched the store, to no avail. The police were called. Someone had seen the boy leave the store. The customer left. In some businesses, that would have been the end. But Allen Hall and the other managers fanned out, combing the blocks around the store, until they found the boy. (He thought his mother had forgotten him, and was trying to walk home himself.) Relieved, the customer said she would never shop anywhere else.

It was pouring rain one day at Store 30 in Miami, and a customer kept coming to the customer service desk asking Lavada Shand, to call a cab for him. But the cab never came. When Lavada went to lunch, she saw that the man was still waiting for his cab to arrive – so Lavada gave the customer a ride to his condominium.

In Winter Haven, deli clerk Talina Evans noticed a customer stranded in the parking lot with a two year old boy. Talina took the customer home. The next day, when Talina noticed a baby shoe in her car that didn't belong to her own son, she stopped by the customer's house on her way to work to drop it off.

In Tampa, a couple came into the Westgate Publix in something of a bind. They were having a birthday party for their daughter, and they needed some supplies in a hurry. Manager Michael Vaughan reacted quickly, telling them not to worry, that he'd take care of everything. Then he *brought the couple coffee* while he gathered everything they needed.

Two days later, the man was on the telephone to the corporate offices. "His smile and his attitude meant everything!" he said. The man told Publix his daughter said it was the nicest birthday party she'd ever had. Then he said, "Men aren't supposed to cry, but hearing my daughter say that made me cry! In 35 years, I've never been in a grocery store like this in America."

The Saturday *after* an Easter Egg Hunt put on by associates of Boynton Beach Store 14, Nancy Conklin was walking through the parking lot at 6 a.m. She watched as a mother and her son got out of their car and walked toward the store with an empty Easter basket.

Somewhat bewildered, the mother asked Nancy where everyone was. When Nancy replied that the egg hunt had been the previous Saturday, the little boy was crushed.

Nancy asked him for his basket and said, "Stay here, I'll be right back." She returned in a few minutes with a basketful of candy and prizes.

One bakery associate took a moment to figure out what would really delight a customer in Lakeland:

> My oldest child is approaching his seventh birthday and as with all family events of this type, I'm running around like crazy, worrying about all the little details. But the one thing I don't have to even think about is the birthday cake. Why? Because I know a lady named Tammy at the Grove Park Publix.
>
> Year after year she has been there helping me with all my weird ideas and last minute changes, for everything from my own baby shower cakes to sympathy cakes for funerals. Like using a little bit of chocolate to darken the children on my daughter's cake (so they would look more like her). But 'thank you' just isn't enough any more. I had to let all of you know how creative and dependable she has been for me, not just once or twice but every time for years. I won't order my cakes from anyone else. She has really earned my business and my trust for some of my family's most special moments.
>
> Lydia Dorsey
> Lakeland, Florida

Jim Bongalis, store manager in Charleston, South Carolina, points with pride to something he observed a young front service clerk doing:

"The Quarter Deck apartments are located a short walk from Store 633," says Jim. "One of our best customers, Ms. Tillman, lives in these apartments. Ms. Tillman comes to the store *every* morning. She is a little slow on her feet and will lean on the shopping cart as she shops through the store. I was coming in the store one morning and saw Gerald Brown, one of our front service clerks, pushing a shopping cart *away* from the store to the end of the shopping center. I was confused by what I saw, and so I asked him what in the world he was doing. His answer delighted me: he had noticed the route Ms. Tillman took each morning, and would leave the cart for her to lean on as she came in each morning. Wow!"

In Covington, young Luke Hudgins noticed that one of his customers was upset, so he asked her what was wrong. She replied that her husband had passed away about a month before. She couldn't even cut her grass by herself. Luke got her address and after work he went to her house and mowed her lawn.

When Cathy Cummings, a store manager in Lake Worth, saw an elderly customer looking distraught, she asked if there was something she could do for her.

"She told me her husband had just passed," says Cathy, "and she didn't know what she was going to do. She had to cook for one. She had to eat alone."

They spoke for a few minutes, then the customer continued her trip through the store alone. Cathy went to the produce department and purchased a bunch of yellow roses for her.

In Port St. Lucie, a customer came through cashier Liz Barton's line with her young son. The boy had his eyes fixed on a Snoopy stuffed animal. When he asked his mother if he could get the Snoopy, his mother replied, "Maybe next time." Liz noticed tears roll down his cheeks.

After the customer had exited her lane, she grabbed the Snoopy doll, paid for it at the office, and ran out to the parking lot, where she handed the stuffed animal to the little boy and watched his tears give way to a smile.

At a Home Depot in Columbia, Jeff Jeup saw some familiar Publix customers trying to put a patio set into their Honda Accord.

"Needless to say," said Jeff, "it was not working very well. I had just got off work and was on my way home so I was still in my shirt and tie. I walked over and asked if they needed a hand, we could put it in the back of my truck. They said no, they lived in Chapin, twenty miles away. I told them that would be okay, I had the time."

Shirley Wilder, a cashier in Stuart, writes:

On April 17, 2004, I saw a customer with four kids get in the check-out lane next to mine. I guess she's a foster mom. One's in a wheel chair, one seems to have difficulty walking, and the other two appear to be healthy. I remembered seeing three of the children at a shoe store, but this was my first time seeing the mother. She too appeared slightly crippled.

While cleaning my register, I was thanking God. I'm a single mom of three beautiful, healthy kids. We are truly blessed.

They checked out through Chris Manco's line. I could see she had a really large order. I continued doing my work and overheard this lady's oldest daughter, about ten years old I'd say, being told to go out to the car and get the rest of her money out of her wallet. The daughter came back and said there was no money left in the wallet. The customer said to Chris, "I'm so embarrassed."

I walked over to see if I could help. Chris said the customer was $19 short. It was 9:50 p.m., ten minutes before we close. The customer said she could either leave, to go get some more money, or just leave some groceries behind. I had $20 in my change purse. I told her she could have it. She said no, she couldn't accept it. I said please, let me help – God has blessed me and I would love to bless you. She agreed.

When Chris recalled the order, the customer was actually $58.61 short. Chris looked at me. The customer said it was too much money for her to ask, and she could leave some of her groceries. But in my heart, I wanted to help. The customer allowed me to pay the balance, and asked what she could do for me.

I told her, "You don't owe me anything. My name is Shirley. Just pray to God to continue to bless me and my family." Then we hugged. I don't even know her name.

I count my blessings every day.

Consider this letter, written by a customer to Publix vice president Tom McLaughlin:

3/6/2004

Dear Mr. McLaughlin:

Where do I begin? I have shopped at your Northgate Square Store in Tampa for some time. The store assistant manager, Mr. Jim Hensley, has made my shopping there, and my family's, feel personal and special. My Mom is ninety-five and I take her there at least twice a week because of the "personal touch" and time that he and his staff give her.

Now, the reason for my taking the time to write this letter is as follows: Mr. McLaughlin, you have a young lady by the name of Cari Musick, assistant deli manager, that did something very special for me, and made a very cloudy day in my life turn into sunshine. She doesn't know me personally, only to wait on my mother and me... She did find out from one of my friends in the store that I recently had cancer surgery. That particular day, I had some disturbing news from my doctor and was feeling depressed.

I went shopping and had to buy some deli products. Cari came out from behind the counter and had a gift bag in her hand. I asked her what is this for? She said she was shopping and saw this and it reminded her of me. So she bought it for me and waited until I returned to the store to give it to me. It was a beautiful angel that had an inscription on the front of it that read, "All things are possible if you only believe."

Mr. McLaughlin, this is above and beyond the service that I am sure you expect of your employees. But it took a burden of worry off my shoulders, and brought tears to my eyes. For this young lady has a heart of gold, feelings that go way beyond taking care of customers. She needs to be given a 'pat on the back' for exceptional caring for Publix customers. I have a new guardian angel in my kitchen, and you have one in your Northgate Square store. She is a priceless employee of the Publix family and should be acknowledged as such.

I re-read what I wrote and am crying again for the sweetness of this young lady. Thank you, thank Mr. Jim Hensley, and thank Publix for having this young "angel" to wait on me.

J. P.
Lutz, Florida

Upon receipt of this letter, Tom sent copies of it (and his response) to the regional director, the district manager, the store manager, and to Cari herself. With her copy, Cari received a "Publix Champion" coin.

How important customers themselves are in producing good service! Customer thanks shown to associates go a long, long way to making associates *want* to care for customers.

Steve O'Brien in Norcross describes how a couple bought a candle to burn the next day, in remembrance of the woman's father who had passed away. After the customers left, Steve noticed the candle still sitting at the register, and headed for the telephone.

"After waking up a few folks with the same last name," says Steve, "I was able to reach the man and offer to bring the candle by on my way home. This really meant a lot to him and his wife. He wrote the corporate office and I received a letter of thanks. It is hard to describe how *appreciated* this man made me feel personally."

When Sophia Russel noticed a customer walking gingerly, she brought her one of the special shopping carts with the bench attached to it and transferred all of the customer's groceries into this cart, so she could sit down.

"She told me how much she appreciated what I did for her," wrote Sophia. "She told me how we take things for granted in life, and how something must happen in order for us to reflect back and notice how important every moment in life is. 'For instance, this moment, thanks to you.' She gave me a hug and a kiss on the cheek and looked me in the eyes and said, 'Thank you, Sweetie.'"

When Sandra Rivera noticed an elderly lady waiting for the Miami STS (Special Transportation Services) to pick her up from the parking lot, she not only drove the customer home and helped her unload her groceries, she also got the customer's telephone number so she could call back to see if everything was okay. When Sandra called her back, the lady said she'd forgotten something in the store, and if Sandra could leave it for her in the manager's office, she'd get it when she next came in.

"I got what she left in the store," says Sandra, "along with some flowers to show her how much we care. When I got to her house and she saw me with what she'd left, she thanked me. Then, when I told her that the flowers were for her, she got all emotional and tears came to her eyes."

15.

Serving Those with Special Needs

*M*aribeth Resen, a resident of Wisconsin, wrote that she'd called Publix in Panama City Beach because her elderly mother – just released from the hospital after a serious bout with influenza -- was still quite weak and unable to drive, or even to stand long enough in the kitchen to prepare food.

"They promptly prepared some food and delivered it to my mother's door," wrote Ms. Resen. "She tearfully told me later that evening that the soup was the first thing she had been able to eat in days. She thought I was wonderful for making this happen for her, but I know that the credit goes to those kind people at the store who didn't stop at policy or established programs in providing exceptional customer service. Hats off to an organization that hires that kind of people and fosters that sort of heart-driven customer service."

Notice Ms. Resen's observation that the store hadn't stopped at policy or established programs. Also recall the statement by Joe DeMartino of Boca Raton, back in Chapter 7: "I wasn't sure if this was allowed, but I figured it wouldn't hurt the store if I went the extra mile for a customer..."

At Publix, the culture is that at the end of the day, seeing to the needs of the customer is *itself* the most important policy. 'If we can do it, why not?" asks Atlanta Division vice president Bob Moore. The attitude Bob describes is nowhere more evident than when Publix serves those with special needs.

Venice customer Helga Mikesell is only 48 inches tall. When she joked with assistant store manager Scott Kiesel about the size of the shopping carts, he took her seriously. Within two days, and with the help of support associates Cathy Plath and Kenny Campbell, Scott had managed to have a shopping cart cut down to Helga's size. The cost was about $250.

When a customer told Joey, the seafood clerk at Store 887, that she was diabetic and wasn't able to eat pasta, he showed her how to use spaghetti squash, instead.

"I thought I was on a Publix commercial," exclaimed the customer. "I kept looking for the hidden cameras."

In Miami, an elderly couple moved in across the street from Store 590 – yet, being homebound, they still called the store and inquired about a delivery service. Store Manager Joann Ferro Albertson offered to do their shopping for them, and to personally deliver the groceries across the street. Following Joann's example, front service clerks Joe Baez and Fritz Dagrin helped the couple clean out and organize their new home. Cashier Jennifer Kraus began going over to their house and doing cleaning for them.

One day while Bill Schmelyun was running the front end, a cashier called him to her register. "When I went over," says Bill, "she pulled me to the side and said, 'This elderly man is trying to pay for his groceries with his keys!'"

"I stepped over to the customer and informed him what his total was," says Bill. "It was only like twenty five dollars.

"He said, 'Take it out of this.' He held up his hand. The only thing he had were his car keys.

"I explained that we needed cash, check, or Presto," says Bill. "He just looked confused.

"Since there was a line, I took out my Presto card, and I paid for his groceries. After his order was bagged, I took him aside, and asked him if he was doing okay. He said his wife had passed away, and he was a little tired. I asked if he would like me to call someone, and he gave me his daughter's phone number. I asked her if she could come get him, and she did."

What about the money?

"I didn't tell her about the register incident," says Bill. "I didn't want him to be embarrassed."

Store manager Paul Hammett recalls a time when he was an hourly associate in Fort Lauderdale. Sister Jean, a nun that Paul knew, asked Paul if he could help a woman who lived nearby. The woman's name was Gladys Gilday.

"Gladys loved creamer potatoes," Paul recalls, "but she would only eat them if they were real small."

Every Friday, before Paul left the store, he went through bags of creamer potatoes picking out the smallest ones. Then he put them together into a single bag and took them to Gladys.

"My coworkers thought I was crazy," said Paul, "but I was determined to get Gladys her potatoes. I even took them to her before going out on dates. Then one Friday, I was bringing Gladys her potatoes and found that there was no answer at her door. I looked through her window and saw Gladys lying on the floor. I called the paramedics and waited with her until they arrived."

As it turns out, Gladys had fallen and broken her hip. Since Paul was her only visitor, she'd spent five days on the floor waiting for help.

"She said I saved her life," said Paul. "She said she knew that if she could just hold out until Friday, she'd be okay, because she knew I'd be there with her potatoes."

After the broken hip, Gladys was hospitalized. The hospital staff made her three decent meals a day, but she still loved her potatoes.

"I made her potatoes and snuck them to her in the hospital," Paul admits. "After she got out and right up until the day she died Gladys told everyone she met how the special attention she'd gotten from Publix had saved her life."

In Nashville, a blind customer calls every week to talk to store associate Marcy Merriman. Marcy spends twenty minutes reading the Publix newspaper ads to her. In Palm Beach Gardens, Bob Asher accompanies a sight-impaired customer during his weekly shopping and makes sure that he gets the right change, since the customer can't see the denominations of bills or the amount of his total bill. In Casey Suarez's district, a customer named Carolyn is unable to drive from the group home she lives in a couple of miles from the store. When Carolyn is unable to have a friend bring her shopping, the team at Store 60 – Jeff, Susan, Vielka and Ivan – do her shopping for her, and deliver her groceries to her home.

Twice each week, there's an elderly customer who walks to the store from the apartments behind Store 685 in Temple Terrace.

"She can make it here okay," says office associate Kristy Castetter "but on the way home, she has to push the cart up a hill, so we always have a front service clerk walk with her. She thanks us every time she comes in. She says she would not be able to make it without our help."

Dealing with senior citizens can certainly be a challenge. But when an associate has the right attitude, seniors can truly be a joy to deal with. There's no better example of that than a story sent along to me by district manager Rob Chapman.

As in many stores, every Tuesday was shopping day at the

Holly Hill Publix for the folks from the local retirement home. These folks would arrive at the store together, by bus, about 9 a.m. The bus returned to pick them up at about 10 a.m.

On one particular Tuesday, the elderly shoppers were finishing up their shopping shortly before 10 o'clock when there was a power outage that caused the whole front end of the store to go down. None of the registers was operational. A wave of panic spread quickly among the 80+ year old customers.

One lady reported that the bus was leaving. Another said it louder. A third began to scream.

"We're going to be left!!!"

The commotion spread through the group, with poor vision and weak hearing aids taking over their logic. The cashiers and front service clerks tried to calm them and tell them it would be okay, but the mounting tension and sheer number of panicking seniors was creating a near-riot. The cries of desperation continued to echo through the speed aisle as little men and women began to walk away from their shopping carts and shuffle to the front in a last ditch effort to escape being left behind.

Dick Crandall, the assistant store manager at the time, saw that the simple shopping trip was turning into a day of terror for his most loyal customers. Realizing that the bus was not in fact about to leave, but that the crowd had been whipped into a frenzy of misinformation, Dick quickly jumped up onto one of the check stands and yelled out to the crowd, "THE BUS IS *NOT* LEAVING!"

Not satisfied with Dick's emphatic statement, one old timer yelled back, "HOW DO YOU KNOW?"

As fast with his wit as he'd been getting to his feet, Dick Crandall grabbed the jangle of store keys hanging from his belt and replied triumphantly, "BECAUSE I HAVE THE KEYS TO THE BUS!"

At this, a cheer went up from the group. Dick was met by pats on the back and hugs from the little widows, who now realized that the situation was resolved: the bus was going to be there until "the manager" said it was alright for the driver to leave.

16.
The Spirit of Service

In 1992, Publix adopted a mission statement. It reads as follows:

Our Mission at Publix is to be the premier quality food retailer in the world. To that end, we commit to be

- Passionately focused on Customer Value
- Intolerant of Waste
- Dedicated to the Dignity, Value and Employment Security of our Associates
- Devoted to the highest standards of stewardship for our Stockholders and
- Involved as Responsible Citizens in our Communities

Notice the last bullet point. "Involved as responsible citizens in our communities." To the person with a sincere service mentality, service to customer and service to community often go hand in hand.

In Nashville, store manager Keith Phillips donated coffee, sugar and creamer to a National Guard unit deployed to the Middle East.

In Orlando, Kris Kolczynski helped with a food give away that fed over nine hundred families Thanksgiving dinners.

In Jacksonville, store manager Brian Haynes was approached by an organization trying to help a homeless man get back on his feet. Brian told the woman to pick out fifty dollars worth of groceries and take them to the register and he would pay for them with his own credit card.

In 1996, the Publix United Way campaign raised over $10 million dollars in donations to the United Way. As a result of this campaign, Publix was honored with the United Way's 1997 "Spirit of America" award, its highest national tribute for corporate community involvement. In the years since winning the Spirit of America Award, the level of contributions to the Publix United Way campaign has only continued to rise, with the 2003 campaign raising over twenty-three million dollars through associate contributions and a match from Publix Super Markets Charities.

In accepting Progressive Grocer's 1998 Retailer of the Year award, Charlie Jenkins Jr. said: "We've put a very strong emphasis on community relations programs. I suppose the United Way is one of the most visible things we do. But it's not a management thing. It's something that belongs to Publix associates."

In 1999, Publix received an Outstanding Industry Partnership Award for contributions to the Food Industry Crusade Against Hunger. In 2001, Publix was inducted into the Special Olympics Hall of Fame, and in 2003, it raised over a million dollars for the Special Olympics. The same year, it raised over two million dollars for the March of Dimes. And since 1995, Publix has raised over twenty-two million dollars for the Children's Miracle Network.

But as Ed Crenshaw points out, "It's more than dollars. It's a matter of people giving their time. We encourage it, and we make sure our people know that we support their efforts."

Publix has never sought to total all the volunteer hours its people have put in for community service and charitable work. But Publix associates donate as much of their time as they do of their money.

In Port Charlotte, assistant grocery manager Jessie Varnam and stock clerk Cornell McCall made a presentation on nutrition to the pre-kindergarten class of a customer's daughter.

In Miami, assistant store manager Kelly Mayo rented a six ton rental truck in order to deliver five hundred turkey and ham deli dinners to the Jewish Community Center. The very next day he drove six pallets of turkeys to Homestead for delivery to migrant workers, loading and unloading the turkeys himself.

At Store 595, the crew has a twenty year tradition of supporting the Thanksgiving Basket Fund. After the 2003 drive concluded, Fund representative Sheila Stieglitz sent a letter of thanks to the corporate offices saying, "I wanted you to know how much I appreciate the wonderful people who manage 'my' Publix."

Craig Fitzpatrick tells about a Jacksonville customer who'd become bed-ridden:

"She had been recently widowed and left with no family to turn to for help," says Craig. "In spite of difficult circumstances, she refused help from her local organizations and was determined to take care of herself. I delivered groceries to her apartment a few times a week, and did odd jobs, like sweeping and cleaning, that she was unable to do for herself. Sometimes, she would call just to talk, because she was very lonely and needed someone to converse with."

"One day she called me with a sad voice and tears flowing to tell me that her cat had died sometime that night. He was on the floor next to her bed where he always slept. I knew how much she loved that cat because all she would feed it was Publix rotisserie chicken. Goodness gracious, that cat ate two chickens a week – I hoped that wasn't the reason it died."

"Anyway," says Craig, "I told her that I would be right over and take care of everything. I called a friend at a local cemetery, and he was nice enough to find some space that shouldn't be disturbed. My friend and I buried her cat within an hour of her call. She was very grateful that we would do such a thing for her."

Then, Craig gets thoughtful. "It wasn't a big deal to me at the time," he says, "but now that I think about it... it really was a big deal."

Of course, there are other people who feel less attached to cats. A lady approached store manager Jason Macklin one night and said she was not sure if there was anything Jason could do, but there was a dead cat on the sidewalk out on South Florida Avenue in front of his store.

"She said it looked like kids had put a sticker on the cat and it made her feel bad," says Jason. Committed as he was to community service, Jason told her he would take care of it. "I walked out to the road with one of the front service clerks," says Jason. "We bagged the cat up and disposed of it in a dumpster."

The customer then wrote a letter to CEO Charlie Jenkins Jr., stating how, in her view, Publix never hesitates to fulfill a request from a customer. Demonstrating the dry humor for which he is well known, when Charlie copied the customer's letter of appreciation back to Jason, he wrote a personal comment on it.

"Jason," said the handwriting in the margin, "that is the first dead cat compliment I have ever received."

It was years ago that B.J. Cure, a grocery department manager in Miami, first decided he wanted to help needy children with gifts at Christmas. He obtained lists of kids in low-income neighborhoods – kids who qualify for free school lunches. He then cajoled donations of gifts from friends and relatives and even Publix customers. Putting on a Santa suit, he delivered the gifts to the schools. What started in the early 90's with a hundred and seventy kids getting gifts has grown to the point that B.J. now collects and distributes over *three thousand gifts* to kids at over forty-five schools and enrichment programs in Dade County.

In Satellite Beach, a customer called ten recycling operations trying to dispose of a large quantity of Styrofoam, but she had no success until she called Publix manager Bob Armbruster, who went out of his way to help her. After describing Bob's assistance, the customer wrote:

> I also want to thank Publix management for making the commitment to helping the community by setting high ethical standards and keeping their word. Having been in this region of the United States only a couple of years, I was not acquainted with Publix, their culture, or what they stood for. However, having heard personal testimonials from several business acquaintances and now experiencing it for myself, *I am coming to understand Publix and their high standards not only as a store, but as a positive force in the community.*
>
> J.P.
> Satellite Beach, Florida

A similar letter was received at Store 392, written by a Title I teacher, thanking the store for its help in marketing a school program. "We were greatly impressed," wrote the teacher, "especially when Wal-Mart, Winn-Dixie and Target had all refused. We all here truly believe Publix is for community involvement. Publix, unlike the others, actually 'walk the walk and talk the talk.' I will always be a Publix shopper."

As with just about everything else at Publix, when it comes to community service, Mr. George led the way. Starting with the George W. Jenkins Foundation (now known as Publix Super Markets Charities), he also supported the Boy Scouts and a long list of other non-profit organizations.

His daughter, Carol Jenkins Barnett, inherited her father's generous nature. In 1995, in her home of Polk County, she was a co-founder of Success by 6, an early childhood initiative that plans and coordinates community resources for parenting and early childhood development. Carol was heavily involved with *Feed Me a Story*, a public awareness campaign that promotes daily reading to children. Publix itself spearheaded the campaign in the southeastern United States, providing television spots and print and radio ads. Carol has also served on the Polk County Citizens Task Force for Children and Families, and was a co-founder of Teen Net, a youth organization that provides activities for Polk County teenagers. She is now also the president of Publix Super Markets Charities.

Carol's husband, Publix vice chairman Barney Barnett, has served in leadership positions on United Way of Central Florida and the United Way of America, Lakeland Economic Development Council, Gulf Ridge Boy Scouts of America, Tampa Bay Partnership, Florida Southern College, the Florida Council of 100, the Lakeland Kiwanis Club, the YMCA, and Volunteers in Service to the Elderly.

In recognition of their service to the community, Barney and Carol together won the United Way's 2002 Alexis de Tocqueville Award. The criteria for this award include commitment to the voluntary system of human service, and inspiration in encouraging others to work hard to help others.[6]

In service to the community, as in service to the customer, Publix leaders have always set an example, and that example becomes part of the company culture.

Publix people also rise to the occasion when individuals, or the community as a whole, are in crisis.

On Merritt Island, eighteen-year-old front service clerk Jake Cowley was returning to the store after carrying out a customer's groceries when he noticed smoke coming from the bottom of a car. Thinking he might be of help, he approached the car and saw that it was *filled* with smoke. He opened the car door, and when he did so, he heard coughing. Jake reached into the car and pulled out three young children from a fire.

In Greenacres, front service clerk Daniel Meighan was bagging for a customer when he noticed the customer's young daughter was choking on a piece of candy. Dan performed the Heimlich maneuver and dislodged the obstruction.

In Atlanta, there was a big fire behind Store 724. Meat manager Jordan Spearman and assistant store manager Joe Schmidt went behind the store to discover several hundred firefighters battling a blaze in an apartment complex on North Avenue. As the fight wore on, the firefighters grew hot and exhausted. Jordan and Joe went back to the store and got several cases of Publix water, nutrition bars, Gatorade, and ice, giving it to the firefighters who were battling the blaze.

---

[6] In receiving the award, Barney and Carol followed in the footsteps of such former winners as comedian Bob Hope and presidents Jimmy Carter and Ronald Reagan.

In Hialeah, associate Jeff DiDonato helped put together five hundred pounds of food for a relief mission to Honduras after the deadly hurricane that hit Honduras in 1998.

In 2004, the City of Sarasota experienced a major water line break. The safety of the city's drinking water was in question. Officials informed residents to avoid drinking the tap water – a major problem for the city's schools. Wayne Glass, who works at the shipping office at the Publix distribution center in Sarasota, decided to become involved. He contacted the necessary higher-ups at Publix and obtained permission to donate twenty-one hundred bottles of water to the schools.

Chuck Fair remembers an evening when he was a common area manager at Store 137 in Tallahassee. It was about 5:30 p.m. when he took a call from Sydell Houston, a common area manager at Store 113. Florida A&M University had received a bomb threat against its cafeteria building, explained Sydell. Unable to feed the students, FAMU wanted several hundred chicken dinners, quick – and Sydell had committed to provide them.

"Between the local Publix stores, we cooked about six hundred three-piece chicken dinners, packaged them, and had them ready for pick-up within a couple of hours," says Chuck. "We used all the potato salad, baked beans, and hot sides we had in stock. Ms. Sandra in the kitchen fried chicken until she dropped! A couple of stock clerks and I trayed up the dinners."

John Boatwright remembers the week before Easter, 2004. "There was a fire burning in the east fork of Wakulla County. The Department of Forestry contacted us on Monday and told us they needed supplies and meals for 225 firefighters. They had checked with the local Winn-Dixie store in Crawfordville and were told they could not take care of their needs. We said we could and would be glad to help.

"The Department's biggest concern," says John, "was feeding the firefighters on Easter Sunday, since our stores would be closed. We told them we'd come in on Easter morning to make their lunches and deliver them to them. They were overwhelmed."

Clayton Hollis was a store manager in New Port Richey when hurricane Elena hit town. At the time, Clayton lived in a condominium on the coast. He was sitting on his porch watching the gulf water as Elena came up Florida's west coast. When the authorities came through, evacuating the coastal residents, Clayton headed for the shelter, as instructed. But later in the evening, watching the television news, he heard the anchorman plead for the store manager of the New Port Richey Publix to get to the store, as the Red Cross needed supplies for the shelters.

Clayton tried to leave, but those in charge of the shelter wouldn't let him. So he went out a different door, claiming he needed a smoke. (He doesn't smoke.) Outside the shelter, he jumped into his Jeep and high-tailed it to his store. Arriving there, he was greeted by his assistant store manager, Henry Pileggi, and his meat manager, Albert Miles. They'd both been watching the same broadcast.

For the next three days, as Elena stalled just off the coast, the three men were prohibited from opening the store for business, and prohibited from leaving the premises. They'd all left their families. They stayed in the store, bagging up food supplies for the Red Cross to deliver to the shelters and for police and fire departments working around the clock.

"We just did what needed to be done," says Clayton. "Besides," he adds, "we could take showers in the mop room, and we watched every video rental movie we had on hand!"

In 2004, four major hurricanes hit Florida in the space of six weeks. 678 of Publix's 829 stores were hit by at least one of the storms – and 617 were affected more than once. After the first of them, Publix set up a relief fund which raised nearly two million dollars. In addition to thousands of jars of peanut butter and jelly, Publix donated more than 30,000 three-pound bags of apples, 100,000 bags of ice, and 70,000 gallons of water to areas affected. Its associates and customers donated an additional twenty-seven trailer loads of product to the Salvation Army and United Way. Publix rented one of its stores to the Federal Emergency Management Agency for six months – for $1 per month. And that was just Publix's response to the *first* of the season's four hurricanes. Long before the fourth hurricane had come and gone, stories began to circulate about Publix associates and how they had risen to the challenge. When the hurricane season was finally over, Charlie Jr. sent out an e-mail to all the stores, thanking them for their service – and including four of the best individual stories he'd heard.

Since 1994, Publix has recognized several associates at its stockholder's meeting with a special award. Known as the "Mr.

George Community Service Award," it's given each year to one associate in each division who personifies the spirit of charitable community involvement demonstrated by George Jenkins himself. The winner receives a trophy, a feature write-up in the Publix News, dinner with the company's top executives, three days off with pay, and a $5,000 contribution to the charity or charities of his or her choice.

At the 2004 Stockholders meeting, I watched the current winners receive their awards and heard what they had to say.

Glenn Fite, Jr. won the award for his work with United Way, the Salvation Army, the Polk County Association of Retarded Citizens (ARC) and Volunteers in Service to the Elderly (VISTE). "We see the positive and the potential in people," he said. "All they need is a little encouragement and attention."

"Baker Bob" Faught was recognized for bringing young people with special needs into his store three times a week to interact and learn about bakery operations. He described the "heartwarming" experience he has every time a person with special needs tells him they love him.

Tim Screws won for his work with the United Way, St. Jude Children's Research Hospital, and Boys and Girls Clubs. Tim said he felt "fortunate to be with a company that *allows* me to participate in help for the community."

Melissa Ellison won for her work with the Charlotte County Healthy Start program, the American Cancer Society, the Muscular Dystrophy Association, and the United Way. She got really choked up as she talked about the look on people's faces when you do them a good deed. And she expressed thanks that the Publix Mission Statement "has given me the avenue and the encouragement to do this."

Finally, Miami Division winner Andrew DeLong founded "Youth Encouragement and Support" ("YES"), a Martin County program dealing with drugs and related problems. Andrew summed up his feelings by saying, "Being asked to help is a privilege. Publix people understand that privilege."

As in prior years, these examples of community service were publicized throughout Publix. Once again, associates throughout the organization were reminded what it is that Publix values most.

A spirit of giving also fosters relationships. Here, a Publix associate helps make a child's holiday special.

Publix caters to all kinds of customers – even the furry and feathered ones. Here, a store in New Port Richey, Florida, announces its annual Pet Picture Day.

During Publix's annual "Take Your Child to Work Day," youngsters get a behind-the-scenes look at customer service. Here, a young artist pictured what she learned.

In 2004, four major hurricanes hit Florida in the space of six weeks. This store in Lake Placid, Florida, distributed free ice to an area hit especially hard.

When a loyal customer joked with Store Manager Scott Kiesel about the size of shopping carts, he took her seriously. Within two days, he had a shopping cart modified to accommodate her needs.

Publix President Ed Crenshaw says that perpetuating the company's culture can only be done by "talking to people one-on-one about their experiences with the company."

Publix's Mission calls upon associates to be involved as responsible citizens in their communities. Here, Publix Chairman Howard Jenkins puts the mission into action.

Publix executives go to great lengths to inspire associates. Publix Vice Chairman Barney Barnett was even willing to kiss an orangutan in order to encourage associate involvement in their communities.

17.
Beyond Fifty

*T*he book *Fifty Years of Pleasure* was published in 1980. It described how Mr. George founded Publix, and how, by 1980, Publix had grown to over two hundred stores. It described the excitement of those early years, and how, after fifty years, Publix had become a successful "big business" with a "family feeling." It could safely be said that Mr. George's strategy had paid off. By keeping his focus on the customer's shopping pleasure, he'd built Publix into a highly successful chain of super markets, focused on great service to the customer and to the community.

Meanwhile, however, as *Fifty Years of Pleasure* made clear, Mr. George's founding vow had been that in *his* company, he'd "go around and visit the stores." When there were two stores, and then nineteen, and then fifty and more, that kind of personal attention was possible. Publix's early growth had been sustained directly by Mr. George's personal presence, his personal commitment, and his personal enthusiasm. But could a "family feeling" exist in a chain that had grown as large as Publix? Could anyone personally visit over eight hundred stores?

Senior vice president Jim Lobinsky has been working for Publix since he started as a youngster in 1956 (bagging groceries). In the summer of 1958, he visited every Publix store. There were only about thirty five of them at the time. It took him only three days. In 1995, he decided to do it again. There were over four hundred stores then. This time, it took him almost *four years* to complete the tour.

It is Jim's intent to visit every new store that opens between now and the day he retires. But he can hardly visit every store every year. There are just too many.

So how did the culture Mr. George created in the 1930's and 1940's manage to continue into the 1980's and 1990's?

The 1980's was a decade of technology. Electronic scanning was rolled out to every store. The first ATM machines were installed in 1982, and by the end of the decade, there were ATMs in every store. But while these innovations did much to enhance the customer's total shopping experience, they did nothing to strengthen, or even maintain, the friendly personal relationships that were also critical to the company's early success.

Upon the death of Joe Blanton in 1983, Mark Hollis became the new president of Publix. Not long into Mark's presidency, Publix took a new direction. In the mid 1980's, Publix made a strategic decision to go into the pharmacy business. And that decision required looking outside the company for trained and licensed pharmacists.

Publix opened its first pharmacy in 1986, in Altamonte Springs. More followed quickly.

From the beginning, the pharmacists at Publix represented something of a different culture from the traditional retail grocery clerk. Pharmacists were highly educated, having to earn advanced degrees to be licensed. And with the whole health care system booming with new drugs, the big pharmacy chains were in a never-ending bidding war for their services. They commanded a relatively large income from their first day on the job. Never mind that pharmacists graduated from pharmacy school in significant debt from student loans, the fact remained: compared to the average grocery clerk, the pharmacists were well-off, educated, and in high demand.

The typical Publix manager started his or her career while in high school. Many began having families and work responsibilities that took college out of the pictures of their lives. They'd been educated not at the university, but in what they like to call "the real world." So it shouldn't be surprising that the meat cutters and grocery people of Publix were at least a little skeptical of the pharmacists. Would these well-paid, highly-educated types be able to give the kind of service Publix expects? After all, the reasoning seemed to go, doesn't good service require a bit of humility? Or, to put it more bluntly: *Can a pharmacist get down and mop a floor to clean a spill?*

Ron Miller began Publix's pharmacy program in 1986. He didn't start out bagging groceries. But despite his pharmacy license, he had the personality of a "regular guy." During eighteen years of his influence, the pharmacists worked hard to maintain the attitude and standards of service that exist elsewhere in Publix. In fact, pharmacists end up knowing a great deal about their customers – who, after all, are their "patients" as well. A special kind of bond can form between pharmacist and customer.

Here's a letter received about Publix pharmacy manager Raj

Toprani:

Every time I have to get a prescription filled I hope that Raj is working. He not only knows my name when I am shopping, he also knows the names of my children. He knows when they are sick and always makes it a point to ask about them.

If Publix recognizes employees for excellent customer service, Raj should be getting the biggest award possible. Please commend the staff at the New Tampa Publix. They are doing a great job.

K.A.
Wesley Chapel, Florida

An e-mail received from a customer in Jacksonville raved about the pharmacy at Store 884 on Touchton Road. "I would like to say that I was an employee of Winn-Dixie for 14 years," the e-mail began. "And the situation I had would have been a half day ordeal at a Winn-Dixie pharmacy.... Upon a recommendation from a family member, I tried the Publix pharmacy. When I arrived at the store around 7:45 p.m., I was greeted by the assistant pharmacy manager, Kim. In less than five minutes I was on my way home with the prescription filled. With all the competition today, it is good to see someone still cares about the customer.

M.T.
Jacksonville, Florida

And a handwritten letter to Store 417 from a cancer patient in Bradenton:

I'm writing this letter concerning your pharmacist, Leslie. I think she is an absolute "god sent." Leslie really means a lot to me. She's very fast and efficient, and can resolve any problem with such kindness, and *always* a smile on her face. Karen and Sophie take good care of me also. But please make sure, if you would, pull Leslie aside, give her a pat on the back, and tell her what a wonderful job she is doing. Because of her, I'll never go back to Walgreens or Eckerd.

Sincerely,
B. J. H.

In Oviedo, pharmacist Karen Zielke brags about the outstanding customer service provided by her pharmacy technician, Cyndi Aho. Karen tells how an elderly woman presented Cyndi with a prescription for a cream that had to be applied to the affected area daily. Karen and Cyndi filled the prescription and Cyndi began to ring up the order at the register. But when the customer looked at the directions on the container and realized that the doctor had prescribed a topical product, she suddenly turned gloomy and perplexed.

"I live alone," the lady said. "How am I ever going to apply this to my back, when there's no one to help me?"

Cyndi didn't miss a beat. She just grabbed a pad of latex gloves and said, "I'll apply it for you in the rest room. And if you need more help, you can come back every day and we'll be glad to see you're taken care of."

Karen says the customer almost cried, she was so appreciative.

Around Christmas time, Pharmacy manager Deb Bonfessuto in Clearwater got a call fifteen minutes before closing, and realizing the customer was feeling bad, delivered medications to the customer's home.

"Even if we have to go out of our way," says Deb, "to our team, that is exactly what it's all about... going the extra mile. Every little bit counts for the care of the patients we serve. To us, they are an extended part of our Publix family."

Alana Kelly, who manages a store in Smyrna, likes to brag on her associate Heather Cargle. Heather is a student at Chattahoochee Tech, studying business management. She also works part time as a pharmacy technician. Heather developed an affection for a customer who was diagnosed with cancer, and before long, Heather was driving her to and from her chemotherapy treatments. Her church youth group raised over four hundred dollars to help pay for the customer's gas, hotel and other expenses for a trip to see a specialist in Tennessee. And when the customer became bedridden, Heather took fresh flowers to her home every day.

In Cocoa, a customer approached pharmacist Grace Rhodes looking for pharmacy manager Jim Eavey. Jim wasn't in the store at the time, so Grace asked the customer what he needed.

It turns out, the customer was simply there to thank Jim. The customer had come in shortly before Christmas about what he thought was bronchitis. After listening to him breathe, Jim said he really thought the man ought to go to the emergency room and be checked out. The customer took Jim's advice and ended up spending all of Christmas week in the hospital being pulled out of congestive heart failure. He said the doctors told him if he hadn't come in when he did, he wouldn't have been around to see the new year come in.

Pharmacist Valerie Gurr of Suwannee provided this story:

> February 9, 1999, started out like a regular day. But that would all change when Tammy Hernandez brought a lady over for some advice. The woman, who we'll call Randi, was experiencing stomach pain and wanted something to make her more comfortable. It was obvious to us that the woman was very pregnant, and in labor.
>
> We brought her behind the pharmacy counter to try to keep her as comfortable as possible, and I called her doctor's office in Dahlonega, about an hour from the store. They kept me on hold for several minutes; all the while I am timing Randi's contractions. By the time they came back to the phone, Randi's water had broken and her contractions were only two to three minutes apart. It was clear there was not going to be time to get her to the hospital, and I called 911. Then we hunkered down to deliver the baby in our pharmacy! Mary Gomez, my technician, ran to get some pillows we happened to have on display. The EMTs arrived in the nick of time, and a healthy baby boy was delivered right in my pharmacy.

By 2004, Publix included over 1,100 licensed pharmacists among its associates. It had been recognized by Wilson Rx as the number one supermarket pharmacy in the nation in customer satisfaction.

The major challenge of the 1980's had been met. Publix had shown that it could develop a major new line of business without sacrificing the Publix culture of service. Indeed, the pharmacies had increased the feeling of loyalty and relationship that exists between Publix and so many of its customers.

By the end of the 80's, the nation's largest supermarket chain -- Kroger – had sold off its Florida Choice chain and left the state of Florida altogether. Publix's pharmacy operation was up and running successfully. A share of Publix stock purchased for $10 in 1959 was now worth $1,600 (*without* reinvestment of dividends).

Everything seemed to be working. Everything seemed to be going right.

But on August 8, 1989, as the decade of the 80's was about to close, a new challenge arose. Mr. George – who had started the company and personally sustained it for sixty years – suffered a stroke that left him confined to a wheelchair. He had lost most of his ability to speak.

Could Publix succeed without the active leadership of the man who, it had seemed to many, *was* Publix?

A letter from a customer in Deland raved about the Publix associates there, then closed with these words:

> I have always felt that the employees of Publix were far and away the most cheerful, the most patient and the most accommodating of any of the super markets. Whatever you are doing is working!

If Publix was going to survive and prosper after Mr. George's stroke, it was vital that the people to whom Mr. George had entrusted the company knew what it took. What *was* Publix doing to make it work?

We'll turn to that question in Part Two.

PART TWO

A PIECE OF THE PIE

18.
Rewards

*W*hen floral clerk Irene Levy in Tampa spent extra time with a bride-to-be in choosing flowers for her wedding, the young lady decided to order her wedding cake from Publix too. When Oakland Park bakery manager Glen Belfer did a great job on a wedding cake, the customer who'd ordered it hunted him down *seven years* later, wanting him to make another. Satisfied customers come back for more.

And *delighted* customers engage in word-of-mouth advertising. When Doug Finley made a home delivery to Mrs. C in Port St. Lucie, he was still standing in the customer's driveway when her sister and some friends pulled in.

"Mrs. C was so appreciative for the delivery," says Doug, "that she held up the packages, bragging to her friends what 'her Publix' did for her. She then went around the car and held up the package, bragging to the neighbor across the street. Her sister's friends were talking between themselves how they just couldn't believe that Publix went out of their way to take care of her."

Raving fans lead to increased sales. Increased sales lead to profits. But do rewards influence people to provide good service? And if so, what rewards?

When Mr. George purchased a nineteen store chain in central Florida called All American Stores in 1945, one of the first things he did was to expand the bonus system. Until then it had included only the manager; once he'd revised it, every full-time associate received a share. Today's bonus system has been enlarged to include even part-time associates who work a thousand hours in a year.

If you ask Publix associates what they like about working at Publix, getting a bonus check at the end of the quarter will often be part of their answer. And if you ask associates why they work hard, you may hear that it helps them get a bigger bonus check.

At one time, I thought that good service at Publix was the direct result of this self-interest. I imagined associates thinking that customer service leads to customer satisfaction, and customer satisfaction leads to increased sales, and increased sales lead to "more money in my pocket… therefore, I should give good service."

To be sure, the bonus is a constant reminder of the tie between company success and associate success. But is it the prospect of increased sales that motivates a part-time floral clerk to lend her own car to a customer? Or a stock clerk to strike up a friendship with an elderly couple? Is it a desire to increase market share? To increase store profits? To get a larger bonus check?

While monetary rewards may help, there are plenty of companies that offer monetary incentives for their employees, and they don't all get good customer service as a result.

Publix associate Edward Bayliss is also an experienced technician for a critical care unit. So when a man collapsed in his store, he was the one summoned to help. Walking through the double doors of the back break room, Edward saw the man lying on the floor unconscious. No pulse, no breath, no natural color. Edward describes what happened:

"Ensuring that my manager had called 911, I proceeded to initiate CPR. After performing mouth-to-mouth on the aged man, I realized that he was by all rights dead. I continued to resuscitate the man until the paramedics arrived and transported him to the hospital.

"The following day, I purchased flowers and a card that I had signed by all the associates and managers and took to the family, who had been at the hospital since the day before.

"A year passed. And on a busy Friday afternoon while I was working in the front office, a customer handed me a tin of what appeared to be Danish sugar cookies and a card. I proceeded to try to ring up the tin of cookies. As I was scanning the item, the customer stopped me and said, 'No, those are for you.'

"With a look of puzzlement I thanked her, but then asked why she was giving me the card and cookies.

"She responded, 'I would like to introduce you to my husband of forty years. I would also like to thank you for saving his life. If it weren't for you, we wouldn't be spending this holiday season together.'

"I'll never forget that November," says Edward, "and how lucky I am to have had the opportunity to have such an impact for that wonderful family."

In Ocala, store manager Jackie Lenz tells a story about Don Fitzwater, an elderly front service clerk. One day Don was taking

119

one of those really big orders out to a customer's car – the kind that fill three shopping carts with groceries. The customer was very appreciative of Don for helping her, and offered him a ten dollar tip. Don told her it was his pleasure to help her and he couldn't accept the tip. The customer insisted, and wouldn't take no for an answer. Finally, Don told her that rather than giving him a tip, she could put the money in her church offering on his behalf.

In Fort Lauderdale, Patti Sardinelli and Bryan Reynolds were instrumental in helping an out-of-town customer recover his stolen wallet. When the customer handed Bryan twenty dollars as a reward, Bryan refused. The customer insisted. Eventually, the money was accepted, but donated to the March of Dimes campaign.

When you've hired as many people as Publix has over the years,[7] you've probably hired every kind of person. There may be a few in Publix uniforms who act in ways designed to delight customers because they'll get a bigger bonus check. But I don't think that's the case for the vast majority. The stories in Part One show that the behaviors that delight customers occur *on the spur of the moment*. They result from the associate's feeling for the customer. A response to a situation a customer is in, prompted by a tear in the customer's eye, or a panic in the customer's voice. Not by a policy manual somewhere. Not because it's good for the company. Not because it may help make a bonus check bigger.

In all my association with Publix people, and in all the interviews done and e-mails reviewed, I just don't see that a profit motive is the reward that triggers the acts which delight the customer. In any case, I doubt that it would be successful at fostering *relationships* unless it was heart felt.

"I measure the success of my day at work by how many people I make smile," says Philip Ortiz, a deli clerk in Lithonia, Georgia. "Both coworkers and customers. Serving people has been a big part of my life and I wouldn't have it any other way. If I could afford to, I would do it for free."

Corky Valentine is a Publix deli clerk. She's had a number of complimentary letters received about her. "I work and live here in Free Home, Georgia and know most of our customers by name," she says. Her philosophy? "Just be happy with the customer. Let them know that you are there for them. It only takes a minute to do a

---

[7] Since its founding, Publix has hired over a million people.

magic trick or get a balloon for children, and get to know a little something about my adult customers."

Remember what customer Jennifer Hernandez said (in Chapter 10) about a cashier who sings to her children: she "seems to enjoy her job, deriving true satisfaction from helping others."

Susan Mullan, an assistant store manager in Miami, tells the following story:

> On Thanksgiving Eve, the store manager and I were approached by a stock clerk who asked for our assistance. The store was on the upswing of business, as people were picking up their last minute shopping for the holiday. An older lady was standing in the back speed lane, holding her hand over her mouth.
>
> At first, we feared she might be hurt or feeling ill, and we quickened our pace toward her. Speaking from behind her cupped hand, the lady explained to us what had happened – she had lost her false teeth. She'd taken them out and was carrying them in her hand and as she turned the corner at the end of the aisle, her arm was nudged by a passing child.
>
> She gestured, trying to demonstrate what had happened. Her teeth, she explained, had gone flying into the air, and had come down on a display of Gatorade. They were now out of sight, but she said she was quite sure the elusive teeth had gone down between the bottles and were out of sight under the Gatorade rack.
>
> We proceeded to take apart the end cap display, as this was the only possible way of retrieving the missing teeth. As we tried to dismantle the display, we found it almost impossible not to upset other busy shoppers – who couldn't understand why we'd chosen such a time to be taking apart a display in the middle of the crowded store – without embarrassing the toothless customer any further.
>
> By good fortune, one of the stock clerks with extremely thin hands and arms was able to maneuver a gloved hand underneath the display to retrieve the valuable item – which was a little on the dusty side. But the customer left happy, able to enjoy her turkey the next day without the aid of a food processor.

Notice the line in Susan's story, "without embarrassing the toothless customer any further," and the line, "the customer left happy." Susan was not thinking, "if I embarrass this customer, it might adversely affect sales," or, "if I can spare this customer embarrassment, she might buy something else from us." Susan's story didn't end, "and this customer left the store with two hundred dollars worth of groceries." It ended with, "the customer left happy." In the hundreds of stories I've heard and reviewed, I could see again and again that the immediate objective of the behavior was not to make a sale, but to make the customer happy.

The more I listened to Publix associates describe customer service, the more evident it became that these people were simply treating others as they'd like to be treated themselves. They weren't shrewd business people calculating how to maximize sales. They were just good, ordinary people acting kindly, in accord with human nature.

At Store 118 in Okeechobee, meat cutter Vinny Morris tells about a customer we'll call "Mrs. P."

Mrs. P. was known as someone very hard to deal with," says Vinny. "But I found out she is a very nice lady. She asked me to get her enough ground chuck to make one cheeseburger. I went and got her one quarter pound and gave it to her. She thanked me and told me she hated to bother me, as she knew how busy I was. I told her I was here for her, and any time I could help her, I would.

"I found out later that she has a sick husband and the only thing he would eat was the cheeseburger. That's been almost six years ago, and she still comes to see me. *It makes me feel good* when I help someone out. I've made a happy customer, and *I've made a friend.*"

In Chapter 10, we saw how associates in Lithonia had developed a relationship with a customer known affectionately as "Mr. B." According to assistant store manager Bette Shaia, "We *truly enjoyed* providing him with the quality service that we as Publix associates are known for." And according to young front service clerk Randall Smith, "Mr. B's shopping trips to Publix not only gave him something to do, but they enriched the lives of the associates he came into contact with."

In Altamonte Springs, an elderly couple who have health problems have given Keith Ellis their home telephone number so he can check up on them, which he does whenever he doesn't see them for more than a few days.   When they're in the store, Keith always seeks them out, gives the wife a hug, and goes to the deli café to chat with the husband about golf or about the man's adventures in the Coast Guard.   Asked why he has become so close with the couple, Keith says it's for selfish reasons.

"It makes me feel good," he says.   "As hectic and crazy as it can get in the store at times, the one constant that makes it all worth while is having this special contact. After all, isn't that the way Mr. George taught us?"

Everyone who's ever brought a smile to someone else's face knows that giving delight to someone else is its own reward. Those who have the "service mentality" know the old saying especially well, "To give is to receive."   Known for his enormous wealth as well as his generosity, Mr. George was once asked how much he thought he'd be worth if he hadn't given away so much. "Probably nothing," he replied.

A person has to wonder how many others Mr. George inspired with that same wisdom.

This immediate satisfaction is the real reward for the acts of courtesy or kindness that mark service at Publix.   It's the real motivator.   The service given is simply a reflection of natural human kindness.

"We are blessed to have associates caring enough about others to go above and beyond in providing premier customer service," says Randy Rigdon, who works in the cabinet shop at the distribution center in Jacksonville.

But is Publix more "blessed" than, say, Winn-Dixie, or Kroger, or Wal-Mart? If good customer service is simply ordinary people acting kindly, then why do objective studies suggest that some companies – like Publix -- excel in this area, while others lag? Did Publix somewhere end up with more "blessing" than other companies? Or are there really business practices that enable or stimulate such kindness?

What does Keith Ellis mean when he says that Mr. George "taught" such behavior?

19.

The Chairman's Umbrella

Recall the 1995 New York Times article quoted in Chapter 3? That article compared Publix to a supermarket operated by Grand Union in New York. It considered what happens if a customer spills a bottle of jelly in a supermarket aisle. The article quoted Frank Margiotta, a spokesperson for the union which represents employees at Grand Union. According to the article, Mr. Margiotta said that union contract work rules do not forbid cashiers from mopping up spills, "but it's just not done – that would be the job of maintenance employees." The *Times* also quoted Margiotta as saying that while customer service problems were sometimes attributed to unionized employees, such difficulties were 'rightly the responsibility of management.'"[8]

Is customer service "rightly the responsibility of management?" In the 1990's the policy of the Safeway and Vons supermarket chains in California required cashiers to smile at customers, and to call them by name. Managers were doing anonymous "mystery shopping" to ensure compliance. The practice prompted a legal challenge by the unions representing the chains' employees. The basis for the challenge was that customers might mistake friendliness for flirtation. By *requiring* employees to exhibit friendly behavior to customers, regardless of context, the companies were exposing the employees to possible sexual harassment by customers. So went the argument against the policy *requiring* clerks to smile.[9]

Can employees be *required* to smile or to use a customer's name? And if so, under what circumstances? I'm sure the lawyers for the companies and the unions made excellent arguments on both sides. But, really – who cares? When friendliness is *genuine*, who needs a rule book to figure out when and where and how?

With the arrival of the new millennium, business scandals were often at the top of the news. Even in the supermarket industry, there

---

[8] New York Times, April 25, 1995. *Shopping Purgatory or Paradise,* by Glenn Collins.
[9] The dispute was eventually resolved on an undisclosed basis.

were reports of accounting irregularities at some of the major chains. Distrust for management was an epidemic. Attitudes toward business and jobs were abysmal.

At CareerBuilder.com, a 2003 study titled "At Work 2003: Past, Present and Future" reported that fewer than half of workers were satisfied with their career progress. Almost 60 per cent of the workers interviewed said they planned to leave their current jobs by 2005. The degree of alienation between workers and their employers has never been greater.

Harper Collins recently published a book by lawyer Stephen Pollan called *Fire Your Boss.* [10] In it, Pollan says that all this alienation is inevitable. He advises readers that fulfillment should come from their personal lives, not their jobs; that a job should be seen as something that supplies maximum income, and that's it.

"The best route to emotional satisfaction is to stop looking for it at work," he says.

How different is the route prepared by Mr. George!

Most organizations are neither sweatshops nor great places to work. Most are in the middle – engaged in trying to achieve their missions; aware that satisfied employees can make a difference; trying to treat their employees well. Trying to convince them that "what's good for the company is good for you." These employers cling to the hope that their employees will find enough fulfillment on the job to stay on board and do their best.

In the 1980's, it became fashionable for American businesses to issue decrees that employees should be called "team members" or "partners" or "associates." Every organization wanted its employees to *feel* like an owner, or a partner, or a team member. But the issue, of course, isn't what people are called. It's how they think of themselves, and how others think of them. Calling somebody a "team member" doesn't get them to *think* like a team member. And merely asking them to think that way – even *pleading* with them – does no better.

But Publix people don't just use different words. There is a real difference. From the time I started working with Publix in 1979, I could tell that Publix "associates" did, genuinely, *think* of themselves (and each other) differently. So when I got a chance to

---

[10] *Fire Your Boss,* by Stephen M. Pollan and Mark Levine. Harper Collins, © 2004.

become an associate of Publix myself, I jumped at the opportunity.

My first clue as to what Publix *did* differently came my very first day on the job. Bill Sneed took me around the company's corporate offices. Bill didn't just say "hello" or "good morning" to everyone he passed. He greeted every person by first name and introduced me to each of them. To Fred, the African-American mopping the floor. To Sally, the blonde watering the plants. To Niecie, the grandmother serving food in the cafeteria. On my first day, I learned that Fred had been a master sergeant in the army. I learned about Sally's love of plants. I learned about Niecie's children. They all smiled at me and wanted to chat.

That afternoon, as I settled in, I wondered: did I belong here? As I ventured out on my own, people smiled and greeted me. Most of them didn't know I was a lawyer, but still, their openness and friendliness threatened me.

Understand: a lawyer is *required to maintain confidences*. To disclose a client confidence, even inadvertently, can give opposing lawyers access to all the communications between the lawyer and the client. As a lawyer, if you let your guard down and leak a client secret, even by mistake, you've struck a devastating blow against your own client. As a result, I'd developed certain habits. I kept to myself. I didn't want people to know who I was, or what I was doing.

Walking through Publix's corporate offices was quite a contrast. It was like the old *Cheers* theme, where "everybody knows your name" (not to mention your family and everything private about you). I felt my very insides churning, inside out, and upside down. Could I ever treat so many *strangers* as if they were my close friends? Or *even*, as the saying went at Publix, like *family*?

At the end of that first day, as I went to leave the building, there was a huge rainstorm outside. One of those windy, dark-sky, pelting monsoons, so torrential that many Floridians lose their fear of hurricanes. It was a hundred yards from the glass door of the building to my car. I was standing just inside the door, looking out, wondering if I should make the dash or wait out the rain.

Hearing a quiet voice behind me, I turned to see Howard Jenkins. *The* Howard Jenkins, chairman of the board. I'd only met him briefly once before. In his hands he had a big green Publix umbrella. He was unsnapping its case, preparing to open it up for his own departure. But when he saw me about to exit, he extended his hand, offering the umbrella to me.

126

"Here," he said. "Take mine."

I declined his offer quickly. Not only was he chairman of the board, but he was my *client*. He was my customer, in a sense. All my understanding of business etiquette required me to decline his kind offer.

But he insisted. "Your car is way out in the parking lot," he said. "Mine is here by the door."

The look on his face, the tone of his quiet voice, made it obvious to me that he really meant it. I thanked him and walked to my car in relative comfort, protected by the chairman's umbrella. Howard dashed to his own car through the downpour.

I didn't think about it then, but it occurs to me, now: Howard's giving me his own umbrella, my first day at Publix. Was it a sign? Were Publix people, simply, used to treating strangers like friends?

Was this how Mr. George had taught it?

20.
The Right Stuff

*M*s. Mary Jean Ziska lives on Florida's east coast, while her mother lives on Florida's west coast. While her mother recovered from an operation, Ms. Ziska made a commitment to help her move a set of bedroom furniture. She arranged for two men to do the loading and unloading, and she rented a U-Haul truck in Palm Beach, which she drove across the state to Naples to oversee the move.

But the two men she'd hired never showed up. Mother and daughter called several friends, none of whom could be reached on such short notice. Ms. Ziska and the U-Haul were due back in Palm Beach by the end of the day. Her mother out of commission, Ms. Ziska couldn't move the furniture herself.

"I was in a panic," she wrote. "Then my mother said she'd call Publix, since they are always so helpful."

I can only guess at what Ms. Ziska must have been thinking. *Call a grocery store for help moving furniture?*

Sure enough. "At first, I was embarrassed that she called you!" she wrote. But her skepticism was unfounded.

"Over and above the call of service, you sent two of your finest Publix gentlemen and hard workers, Mike Ferrer and Nicholas Chery. They were excellent! Not only did they unload the heavy bedroom set -- they even offered to put it together for me! You saved the day for me!

"Mr. Hamilton, I couldn't have done it without your help and I thank you so very much for your kindness and consideration. Not only is 'Shopping at Publix a Pleasure' but knowing Publix hires such great, capable neighborly and professional people is so much more than just a pleasure... It *IS* Publix!"

Chris and Jenny Masters live in Lavonia, Georgia. It's a small town with a population less than two thousand people. The closest "big town" is Toccoa, Georgia –population: 8,226. Toccoa is some twenty miles away.

The Masters family used to do their grocery shopping in their hometown stores, but they couldn't always find what they needed.

When I asked about turkey cutlets, one of the meat counter workers at your competitor commented, 'This isn't New York.'

Finding that attitude frustrating, we decided to come home and telephone the nearest Publix, which happens to be over twenty-five miles away in Anderson, South Carolina. A very nice gentleman in the meat department there told my wife that while he was out of the cutlets, he would butcher a turkey breast for us, if that would fit our needs. When we arrived at the store, his attitude proved to be as helpful as over the phone. Because of his attitude and the selection in your store, we decided there is no reason to waste our time in our local stores any longer. By the time we look, ask, etc. in Lavonia or Toccoa, it is just as quick and much more satisfying to go to Publix and deal with professionals.

Thank you for the training or careful hiring or whatever it is that made the difference in how your butcher treated us versus how your competitor's did.

Chris and Jenny Masters
Lavonia, Georgia

In 2001, Publix store manager Ken Jelonek received a similar comment:

You are to be congratulated for your employment and management policies. What wonderful people you select and how well you train and motivate them. I am retired now but as a business school graduate and former management consultant, I appreciate what you have done.

H. and B. D.
Clermont, Florida

Alabama customer Sandra Masters sent a letter to Publix complimenting the service she'd received from stock clerks Shane Heineman and Tomas Christensen. Ms. Masters concludes: "I am a Director of Nursing at St. Vincent's hospital here in Birmingham and acutely aware of the impact of friendly, respectful, and courteous customer service. *Congratulations on hiring great people and coaching them to be great employees.*"

These are just three of the many letters in which customers have applauded Publix for its hiring practices, employment policies or training of associates.

Let's take a look at those practices at Publix, and inquire how they contribute to customer service at Publix.

Publix long ago made a strategy decision to provide carry-out service to customers' cars. This "investment" in making shopping a pleasure frees up the cashier to focus on scanning, so that customers move through check-out aisles more quickly. It contributes to shopping pleasure. But not a single customer letter I reviewed mentioned speed of check out as a reason for the customer's letter. And while many letters talked about what associates said or did *while* providing carry-out, only a tiny fraction – maybe one per cent – complimented Publix for the fact that it was provided.

Staffing the stores to provide carry-out service – and to keep check out lines open – seems to be something customers *like*, but those practices don't get mentioned when customers write the company to *rave* about the service they've received. Surveys show that *slow* check-out lines are frequent sources of *dis*satisfaction. But providing faster checkout speeds may not be the kind of thing that makes "raving fans."

As we've seen, what generally makes raving fans at Publix is a *personal* experience, one in which the associate genuinely cares about the customer.

"Thank you for hiring such friendly people" is a comment seen again and again in customer letters. What does Publix do to hire people who are more caring than average?

There are a few jobs at Publix (like baker and meat cutter) which require skills gained only through experience. But most jobs at Publix require no specific prior experience or specialized skill. For most jobs, Publix's hiring managers rely mostly on the applicant's answers and demeanor at the time of the interview. They try hard to hire friendly people.

So do these efforts pay off? Are Publix associates friendlier than the employees of other organizations?

I believe they are. The objective ratings and surveys prove it. But the reasons may surprise you.

First, because Publix promotes from within the company, it does little hiring from outside the organization, except into part-time positions.

The following pyramid shows the number of associates at a typical Publix.

Store Manager (1)

Assistant Store Manager (1)

Department Managers (6)

Assistant Department Managers (6)

Full-Time Associates (45)

Part-Time Associates (90)

As the chart shows, there might be ninety part-time associates assigned to a typical store, and only forty-five full-time associates. But this doesn't mean most of the people you see when you walk into the store are part-timers. In fact, since a full-timer works a lot more hours, chances are that in a given store, at a given hour, there will be as many full-time associates working as part-timers – or more.

But let's focus on those ninety part-timers, and consider also the notoriously high turnover in the supermarket business. Publix hires roughly fifty thousand new associates a year to fill ten or fifteen thousand openings. Over thirty percent of the part-time associates Publix hires on a given day will have left the job within three months; over half will have left within six.

The vast majority of this turnover is *voluntary* turnover. In fact, more than ten times as many employees leave of their own accord as get released by Publix.

So when we talk about turnover, we're talking mostly about associates who assess their new jobs and decide it isn't right for them. We're talking about a process of *self-selection*.

From their first days on the job, new associates are immersed in a culture of customer service. Friendliness surrounds them. People are greeting each other, asking about each other's families. Not only managers, but full-time associates – their "peers" – are talking to them about customer service. And if the newly hired associate would rather work on a construction site or in a library, he or she resigns.

Managers do, of course, assess associates. They give new associates detailed feedback on their performance. But mostly as a result of *self-selection*, those part-timers who remain at Publix, and who do a good job, and who want full-time employment, are the ones remaining when a full-time opening occurs. So the part-time associates hired every year do a tremendous amount of *self*-selecting.

Mr. George was once asked, "Is there a certain kind of person who seems to fit in more naturally at Publix?" Mr. George replied, "Well, it's hard to accurately define it, but yes – it would be someone who *likes* the retail business, *likes* meeting people, and has some ambition and wants to work."

Ed Crenshaw describes the key attribute of Publix associates not as an ability, but as "a *desire* to please, a *desire* to satisfy the customer's needs."

"I love what I do," says Tony Parkins, a cake decorator in Atlanta. "Taking care of customers, making them feel their problem is my only concern, is my way of giving 110%. I keep a good spirit about me, so the customer can feel the Publix bakery on Piedmont is a great place to shop."

Vice president Bob Moore says the difference in Publix people is simple: "We love it!" he says. "We love the business, the company, and serving the greatest customers there are. Everyone talks it; Publix people walk it."

Publix's front-line workforce consists not so much of people who have been selected because they are *able* to do the job, but who choose to work there because they *want* to do the job.

That means people who *like* the kind of culture that Publix encourages:

People who *like* to develop relationships.

People who *like* to delight customers.

It's common for experts to lament the high cost of turnover. But the fact is that by hiring large numbers of people, and letting

132

voluntary turnover and a service culture determine who sticks around, Publix is made up of people who really *enjoy* what they do. They are the foundation ingredient – the "right stuff"– in Publix's recipe for superior customer service.

Nearly all of us have the ability to provide great customer service. At Publix, it's less about ability than it is about desire.

As vice president Todd Jones is fond of saying, you "gotta wanna."

21.
Tending to Culture

*I*f self-selection is the first reason Publix associates tend to be friendlier than most, what are the others?

"George Jenkins ran the company pretty much well into his 80's," says president Ed Crenshaw. "He ran the company day to day. I think that's one of the reasons for the success of this company. We had the people that *built* the business *run* the business for a long time. That really gave them a chance to train the new people to come in."

As so many customer letters assert, Publix does a great job of training its associates on standards of service. Newly hired associates attend formal orientation when they begin work. Newly promoted managers go through several days of concentrated training for new managers. Todd Jones talks about the importance of training new people. "New stores, great products, modern innovation – they're each a 'must' in this business," says Todd. "But each pales in comparison to the competitive advantage of our associates. In the food war we are in, the last survivors to stand will be the ones with the best-trained associates."

The formal training that's been developed at Publix is excellent. But when a company is hiring fifty thousand new people every year, it can't afford for much of that "training" to be in formal classroom settings. In fact, the vast majority of the "training" given to Publix associates comes from on-the-job mentoring that new associates get from other associates in the stores. Not from corporate training facilitators, not from full-time trainers based in the stores, but from their fellow associates. Managers training non-managers. Full-timers training part-timers.

Put simply, training at Publix is largely a *cultural* phenomenon.

"I have to tip my hat to all of our store managers," says Ed Crenshaw. "And to the management teams. Because it's up to them to do it. I don't ever think for a minute that a video can do that alone. Sitting people down in front of a video monitor and asking them to watch something on a TV screen and expect that we're going to transfer the culture of the company – by talking about it – well..."

So, how do line managers and co-workers train?

They don't stand and give speeches. They don't point to flip charts. They don't hand-out workbooks.

"It can only be done," says Ed, "by people living it and experiencing it and talking to people one-on-one, first hand, about their experience with the company."

What Publix people do, they do quite naturally, and sincerely, and persuasively. First, they demonstrate the behaviors themselves, setting examples. Then they tell stories.

Like the story Jim Rhodes told me about cleaning the over-pizza-ed oven.

Like *all* the stories shared with me as I set out to write this book.

These are the stories that get repeated, week in and week out, among the people at Publix. It's something they enjoy. It's something they have in common with each other. It's something that sets them apart.

Todd Jones tells this story about his early days as a store manager in Orange City:

> When I relocated, I was told that some of the customers in this area were a little "difficult." I wasn't worried, since I cared so much about our customers. As time passed, there *were* a few customers who were difficult to please, but this only made me want to work harder at winning them over.
>
> One day, a couple came to the customer service counter asking for a refund on a plant they had bought, which had died. They had planted it, gone up north for six months, and upon returning, discovered the plant was dead.
>
> Go figure.
>
> I saw this situation as a great opportunity to "win" over this customer's confidence in Publix.
>
> You see, early in my Publix career, Mr. George had come to a training session I was a part of, and left me that day with one of the most memorable stories I have – one which shaped my professional beliefs. After speaking to the group for a few minutes, Mr. George said, "Here is my home phone number. If there is ever a customer you can't take care of, give them my phone number – because *I will!*"
>
> Back to my Orange City customers. I bought them a new plant. I took it out to their house. *And I planted it for them.*

We ended up being great friends. And I never had a complaint from them again.

Just like a plant will die if not tended, having the right stuff – associates who *like* serving customers – isn't enough if left alone and ignored. The ground has got to be watered. The crops have got to be fed. Good service at Publix is a matter of culture.[11] It has to be tended carefully. "Cultivated." Trained.

But what does that training consist of?

After Chip Broderson was complimented by a customer for how well he'd cared for the customer's mother, Chip's district manager asked him to share his story with other store managers in his area, as part of what it means to be "involved as responsible citizens in our communities." This kind of testimony and story-telling is what sustains the Publix culture.

An essential part of the Publix culture is Publix's commitment to promotion from within. As a result of that commitment, part-timers who like what they do, and do it well, get promoted to full-time status. Many go on to become managers, having already seen or heard stories their managers have shared. Then, they themselves become the managers who set the examples and tell the stories.

Almost all companies have written policies supporting promotion from within. I once heard Charlyn Jarrells Porter, a senior vice president for Wal-Mart Stores, describe Wal-Mart as a company with a "strong" promote from within philosophy. But according to Ms. Porter, only two-thirds of Wal-Mart managers started with Wal-Mart as hourly associates. This is probably typical of companies with "strong" promotion-from-within cultures. But Publix's culture of promoting from within is not just "strong." Virtually 100% of Publix managers started with Publix as hourly associates. Even though there's never been a written directive from the founder, the Board, or anyone, requiring it.

By the mid-1990's, in an effort to support its growth into Georgia, South Carolina and Alabama, Publix was promoting over

---

[11] Sometimes, people think the word "culture" is about eating gourmet foods or going to shows at the opera. But the real meaning of "culture" is the meaning in the word "agriculture." "Cultivation" of a field begins with clearing the land, then tilling the soil, then planting, and watering -- putting the field to good use for the production of crops. Good service at Publix is a product of this kind of culture.

two thousand associates a year into department and assistant department manager jobs. Management positions going unfilled because of a lack of qualified candidates to fill them. Analysts voiced concerns – would Publix be able to train and develop enough new people to manage all these stores? But Publix has maintained its tradition. As in the past, Publix today would rather have a management position go unfilled than to put someone in charge who's unfamiliar with Publix culture and Publix standards of service.

In my experience, this level of adherence to a culture of promotion from within is unparalleled. What's the impact of it?

Craig Lombardi needed a cake and a bouquet for a business party at the last minute. He walked into the Publix store in Conyers, Georgia and immediately encountered problems. First, it was late in the day, and when he got to the bakery, there was no one there to help him. In a hurry, Craig picked up a ready-made cake, even though it wasn't exactly what he wanted. Then he made his way to the floral department to get his bouquet. Once again, he found no one in that department to help him. Once again, he picked a ready-made arrangement, though it wasn't what he'd really had in mind. He'd been hoping to get some small place cards made up, but could find none. So as Craig went up to the customer service counter, he was more than a little disappointed.

But Craig ended up sending an e-mail to the corporate offices raving about the service he'd received. Why?

"I went to the customer care counter and a gentleman named Kenny was there," wrote Mr. Lombardi. "I expressed some disappointment, and he immediately took charge of the situation. He took my cake to the bakery, re-decorated it himself, and was even able to write a message on the cake! He also fixed up a much larger bouquet of flowers, and found the cards I needed. Then he rang me up! Although I was first disappointed thinking no one was there to help me, I sure didn't leave feeling that way! Who knew that in this day and age, someone who worked at "Customer Care" really did care, and was very able to multi-task! Hats off to Publix if the rest of your people are people like this one!"

As Mr. Lombardi's letter reflects, Publix managers don't manage from behind closed office doors. They've not only been promoted from within, they typically have rotated through a number of jobs. They have done, and can do, most of the tasks in the store.

The unwritten, unarticulated Publix philosophy for years has been that every manager needs to understand the business intimately – and the best ways to learn are by doing, and by learning from those who've gone before.

One manager recently told me of a time when a mistake made by his store had really set a customer off. The customer was in his face, angrily waving a finger at him, carrying on well past the point he was used to. He was on the verge of exploding.

Then, he says, he noticed other associates watching. "I realized they were all going to take a lesson from whatever they saw me do. And I kept saying to myself, 'do what Mr. George would have done.' Somehow, I managed to keep apologizing to the customer. By keeping my own cool, I eventually had the customer calmed down, and I took care of him. The customer left satisfied. My crew couldn't believe I hadn't lashed out at the guy. But you know, they told me they thought I'd handled it extremely well. I felt good about not losing my temper, and good about satisfying that customer. *But mostly, I felt great having been able to give my people a good example.*"

Michael Smithkey, a full-time grocery clerk, describes how he watched a young part-timer getting asked by a customer where an item was located. The young man didn't simply tell the woman where the item was, but took the customer with him, showing her where it was on the shelf. Then the part-timer described for the customer a recipe she could use to experience the item at its best.

Though not yet in management himself, Mike was delighted. Then, Mike saw the part-timer turn to the woman's young son and say something that made the youngster laugh. Intrigued, Mike watched the young associate go to the produce department, make a balloon, and bring it over to the customer's little boy.

What did Mike do? He sent the corporate office an e-mail, identifying and bragging about the young part-timer, whose name, he was careful to point out, was Daniel Stedem.

So full-time Publix associates – managers and non-managers alike – look out for this kind of attitude and behavior toward customers. It's what gets noticed among part-time workers. It's the main thing that determines who, among those interested in a full-time job, gets offered one.

"Ideal employee-customer relationships cannot be accomplished without a sincere interest in your employees as real people," said Mr.

George. In other words, cultivating the culture is another thing that stems from simple caring about others.

Bill Fauerbach, now the vice president of the Miami Division, recalls how a wheel-chair-bound Mr. George used to visit Miami even after suffering his stroke. "Once I picked him up at the airport in Fort Lauderdale and headed north on I-95," says Bill. "He motioned for me to turn around and head for Miami. As difficult as it was for him to spend an entire day visiting stores, he always had a smile at the end of the day because he was able to visit with his associates. He would love for them to come up and hug him. Even though he could not speak, his face would brighten up and he would break into a big smile."

Bernadette Viens tells a story about her experience as a shopper in Bonita Springs:

> One day, about twenty years ago, I stopped at the new Publix on U.S. 41 in Bonita Springs, Florida, to get a dozen eggs. It was a lovely new store with a blue tile roof, lots of banners and streamers, and balloons for the kids. I just needed eggs, so I decided to carry my one-year-old, hold my two-year-old's hand, and instruct my four-year-old to hold onto my shorts as we crossed the parking lot.
>
> Since I "just needed eggs," I didn't get a cart. I quickly made my way to the dairy section.
>
> Out where we lived, the only grocery store prior to Publix opening was a Winn Dixie. So my surprise at such a nice clean grocery store was very evident as I looked with awe at the displays and well-stocked shelves. The people working there were quite pleasant. They asked on several occasions if I needed a cart to put my kids in. I'm quite sure they were wondering where I would put my groceries, but I hadn't thought of that yet, since "I just needed eggs."
>
> I got the eggs, but I had to delegate the holding of my two-year-old's hand to the four-year-old so I could carry the eggs to the checkout.
>
> As I approached the line, the cashier grabbed the eggs to help me and rang me up. A nicely dressed man, Damian Minko, the assistant store manager, came to the end to bag my "groceries" and offered to carry "them" out for me. Since I "just had eggs," I declined his offer.
>
> But Damian said, since I already had my hands more

than full, he would carry them out! Not only did he carry out my one dozen eggs, he held my four-year-old's hand and got three balloons – and waited while I loaded everyone into their car seats!

As I look back over my fifteen year career with Publix, I have to say, that manager didn't just help me out to my car that day – he won me over for life.

Bernadette, whose first exposure to Publix was in Bonita Springs, wound up helping Publix break new ground in Atlanta. Bernadette is now the assistant store manager in Decatur. I'm sure she's telling new associates what an impression Damian Minko made on her that day.

That's how the Publix culture spreads. *That's* how "Mr. George taught it."

People demonstrating what customer service is all about. And then, people telling stories about it.

Outside Ed Crenshaw's office in Lakeland is the Publix real estate department. One of the women who works there is Charlene Prine, who used to work in the stores. Ed says he can never pass Charlene without remembering, gratefully, that she was the one who taught him to scan groceries years ago.

Referring to Charlene and the others who guided him along in his own career, Ed says: "Every one of these people took me under their wing and helped teach me the business. From a store manager I worked with, and a District Manager I worked with, everybody was out there helping me become successful. And to me, that's part of this Publix culture that a lot of people don't realize. I think it goes on every day in our company, where people are actively working hard to help other people become successful. That's really what's perpetuated the company, because that's what's built the culture. Particularly over the last ten years, where we've had this rapid growth. That's the only way that that growth could have taken place. We had people that were ready to assume greater responsibility, because someone took an interest in them."

Four months after Barbara Murray wrote the company to compliment store manager Rick Harden, she wrote the company a second time:

When I recently mentioned how pleased I was with the customer service at this store to an employee helping me out with my groceries, he said, "That's nothing. This manager once went to a lady's house and cleaned her floor because, as she was bringing in her groceries, a syrup bottle fell out of the bag and broke in her kitchen."

Think about it. A customer raves to a clerk about a manager, and the clerk raves back, saying "That's nothing!" and sharing a "*better*" story of service by that manager.

It's about managers setting examples. That's what Howard had done when he gave me his umbrella. That's the way new associates grow. That's the way the culture thrives.

It's the second reason that Publix associates are friendlier.

22.
Spices and Herbs

At the beginning of the 1980's, fewer than ten per cent of Publix managers were women or minorities. By 1993, it was twenty-seven per cent. By the year 2003, women and minorities accounted for over forty-five per cent of Publix managers.[12]

We know that diversity is not just about race and gender. As diverse as the world is, with so many unique people in it, there are as many ways to assess diversity as there are people – and maybe more. People of different ages and faiths, people with disabilities, people with different sexual orientations. Floridians and Georgians. Pharmacists and traditional grocery people. Like an infinite variety of flavors, *each* of us represents an example of diversity.

So how does diversity affect customer service? Again, let's get the benefit of the purple potato perspective. The first story is from a Publix retiree:

> I was the assistant store manager at the 100th Publix when it opened in 1963. A great time in Publix history. I've thought about it many times.
>
> Mr. Jenkins staffed this store with some of the best folks he could. After all, this was the big 100th store. A milestone.
>
> Harold Hitchcock – "Bump" to his family and friends – got his first store manager's job when this store in Winter Haven opened. Bump was hardly new to Publix. He had worked with Mr. Jenkins from the time the first new Publix was built in Winter Haven in the 1940's. But he was an untested new manager. When the 100th store opened, Bump was over sixty years old. Could he handle the pressure?
>
> The answer was Yes.
>
> This story is mostly about Harold, but it is also about the way Mr. Jenkins went about looking after his long-time

---

[12] EEO-1 reports filed with the U.S. Government in 1981, 1993, and 2003, respectively.

employee and friend. This was not just for Publix's success, but for Bump Hitchcock's success also.

Jim Lawhun
Retired

Denise Plan, an associate in Birmingham, Alabama, writes about one of her fellow associates:

I would like to tell you about the demonstrator here at Store 882. A very vibrant eighty year old little lady who just poked her head in the door one day, before the store opened, to "take a peek." I was sitting at the table and I asked her if she was here to apply for a job. She replied, "Oh, would you consider giving someone as old as me a job?" After chatting with her for a few minutes, I told her there was a position that would be perfect for her. She had the brightest smile and bubbliest personality – I just knew she would make a great demonstrator.

From the day she was hired, she really became the store ambassador, not only to the customers, but to the other associates as well. At grand opening, she was at the front of the store, giving out samples of the tangerine juice from the produce section. She made every customer feel like a welcomed guest in her home.

In the days that followed, customers overwhelmed us with compliments about her. She did not do her job for the compliments; she did it out of pure kindness and consideration for people. She became the hit with everyone in the store: the kids, the associates, the vendors, and all the customers. When she demonstrated the pies, she would sell so many that the bakery couldn't keep the pies ready fast enough. She truly had a knack with people.

It's with much sadness to have to tell you that we the associates and customers lost our beloved demonstrator. Mrs. Marie Mason passed away on January 29, 2004. When I visited her in the hospital, the only thing she could talk about was getting back to what she loved best, her job at Publix. She said, "If I can just get well enough to come back to work, I know that being around the associates and the customers will heal me."

Her famous thing to say was, "Coming to work every day is like giving a party where I get to serve all my guests the finest treats that Publix has to offer." Then she would laugh and add, "All for free!"

Mrs. Marie will be missed by all here at Publix, but we are all a little better for knowing her. She set the standard for us all to follow in customer service.

In the spring of 2004, a customer e-mailed the corporate office about an experience in a Sarasota store:

> I was leaving the Publix store and backing out of my parking space when I noticed one of your many older food baggers heading briskly toward my car. I had left behind a 2-liter bottle of soda and he was chasing after me to bring it. I didn't get his name, but his action is typical of the friendly service I have come to expect at your store.
>
> D. K.
> Osprey, Florida

In October of 2002, Publix was one of four companies in the nation to receive the Outstanding Employer of Older Workers award from Experience Works, a Washington based organization that recognizes work achievement by older workers.

Meanwhile, in Winter Haven, another customer stopped store manager Richard Harris and began to rave about the service she gets from "Sir Francis." "Sir Francis" (whose last name is McKinnon) is a seventeen-year-old front service clerk.

The customer told Richard: "Far too many times, when you go into a store, the person waiting on you sounds like a robot when they tell you to have a nice day. But not so with this young man. He always knows the right thing to say. No matter what kind of day I've had, or how tired I am, he always leaves me with a smile on my face."

In Naples, Mark Tessier attributes a significant increase in pharmacy sales to the addition of a Spanish-speaking pharmacy technician at Store 516. And nearby Store 781 has a significant mix of customers who speak either Spanish or English. The language barrier sometimes creates problems. But one associate, Veronica Lopez, is deaf and mute. She carries a tablet with her and communicates with customers who seek her assistance in finding products. Store manager Mark Bradman uses her as a positive example in meetings with his associates.

"With all those challenges," he says, "it makes the excuse of language barriers evaporate with others around her."

In Seminole, an African-American customer came into the store looking for fat back. She looked throughout the store herself, and didn't find it. She asked several associates, and they didn't know what it was. It wasn't until the customer asked Lora Adams, deli manager, that she got the help she needed. Lora, an African-American, knew exactly what the customer was talking about. She walked the customer straight to the item and offered her ideas for different ways to use it in recipes. And in Lilburn, African-American manager Olivia Slater is frequently approached with questions about hair care products for black women, while black pharmacy manager Mervin Williams gives black customers with high blood pressure detailed information about why the condition is more prevalent among African-Americans, and what they can do about it.

In Columbus, Monika Wiggins was working the express lane when some customers asked her for a recipe. They were about to host a guest they'd met in Germany; they wanted to surprise their guest with an authentic recipe for Glue Wein. Being German herself, Monika knew Glue Wein well. (It's a holiday concoction of spiced, warm wine.) Getting someone else to cover the express lane, Monika took the customers all around the store, gathering the ingredients and sharing stories of Germany during the holidays.

In Naples, Wayne Herbert's Downs Syndrome hasn't kept him from giving great service at Publix for the past ten years. "Numerous customers shop just to see Wayne's endless smile and welcoming hugs for those he knows (and some he does not)" says store manager Mark Bradman. "He is boundlessly optimistic. In a way, I consider myself his customer. In all the years I have worked for Publix, I learned more from him than anyone else. Humility, sincere appreciation, optimism and a genuine sense of caring for his fellow associates."

And in Columbia, Amy Bundrick is a special needs adult who bags groceries at Store 883. She is very involved in the community. "I go the extra mile to help people and make them happy," says Amy. "I gave a tour to some special education students. It shows that I care about people and care about their needs. I also like people that are regulars, because I know the way they like their groceries bagged. It makes me feel good to see one of my regulars in the store, and they know me.

"Basically, customer service means that the customer is number one and you should do anything for them. You also treat them with the respect that they deserve."

Mr. George believed in giving people opportunity. His generosity included sharing not only ownership, but leadership, with others.

"One of the most important lessons I've learned in my business career," he once said, "is that no man puts together an organization on his own."

"No longer were people just working for the company," according to one writer. "They were working for themselves, and for each other. And one by one, associates grew to realize what Mr. George had known from the start: by giving opportunity to all, they were giving a future to themselves."[13]

In 1997, Publix began a new annual award, named the President's Award. It honors the district manager in each division who most demonstrates success in achieving equal opportunity goals, maintaining a work environment which values diversity, and demonstrating dedication to the dignity, value, and employment security of associates. In 1998, Publix announced the winners of its first President's Award – district managers Barbara Batchelder, Jim Herring, Jim Bushee, and Charlie White. There have been winners every year since.

There are those who say that diversity's good for business, because a variety of perspectives gives a company an edge in understanding customers' needs.

There are those who say that supporting diversity is simply the right thing to do.

But upon reviewing hundreds of customer service stories these past few months, an additional benefit of diversity occurred to me – one that may have more to do with success at customer service than any of the others. If customer service is about striking a chord – if possible, a personal relationship – with customers, then ask yourself: do you ever know who it is who may have that special touch, that unique approach, which will strike the right note with the next customer that walks in the door?

---

[13] *The Pleasure of His Company, The Life and Work of George W. Jenkins.*

A diverse workforce gets people used to being with people not exactly like themselves. It opens them up. And it increases the chance that *someone* in the store could be the one holding the key to the next customer's pleasure.

Sixty-five year old meals clerk and "chef" Don Hogan writes:

> It was a hot summer morning in Marietta when a young lady wearing a baseball cap checked out at our store. After bagging her groceries I stepped behind the cart and said, "I will follow you to your car."
>
> Her reply, "*I* can do it," caught me off guard.
>
> I said, "Ma'am, I'm not questioning your ability, but this is Publix, and I'm here to serve you."
>
> After a brief moment of thought, she replied, "Just this once."
>
> While walking to her car, I observed she was walking with a slight limp. I did not want to presume her physical condition, but I wanted to see if she was alright. I said to her, "My Mom would say you're walking a little gingerly. Are you okay?"
>
> Immediately she paused and proceeded with the following story.
>
> She told me she was vacationing in another state when her car was side-swiped by an eighteen wheeler. She had suffered a broken arm and leg, three fractured ribs, and injury to her lung and liver. She began to tell me, "I don't know why I'm telling you this, but you haven't heard the worst yet..." She removed her cap to reveal a scar along her hair line. This, she said, was the result of a fractured skull. She'd had to have plastic plates inserted into her forehead.
>
> Immediately I removed my chef's hat and said, "What progress medical science has made! Thirty-five per cent of my head above my eyes is sterling silver from a car crash when I was twenty years old."
>
> She started to weep and I said, "Pardon, have I offended you?"
>
> "No," she replied. "I have prayed that God would show me physical proof that he would heal me – and you're the evidence he's provided for me."
>
> This lovely woman used to shop at Kroger and has been

a loyal Publix shopper since our encounter. This just goes to show that all you have to do is take the time to listen to your customers and respond back to them.

True enough. But could anyone else have done as good a job as Don?

A diverse workforce multiplies the potential to develop genuine *relationships* with the greatest number of customers.

23.
A Piece of the Pie

*Y*ou'll recall Mr. George's words describing the opening of the first Publix: "Returning to Winter Haven, I turned in my apron, took the money I had saved to buy a new car, about $1,300, and in 1930, opened my own store next to the one I'd left."

Those words, "my own store," must have sounded good to Mr. George. As he felt the urge to make his store better than any other, he must have asked himself how to get those who'd be working with him to feel the same way. We know that he sold four shares of stock in his new company to each of the two men who'd come with him from Piggly Wiggly. As described in *Fifty Years of Pleasure*, he hired six other employees to work in his store. Since they made only $15 a week, they couldn't afford to buy stock. But Mr. George found a way to make them stockholders too.

"I gave 'em each a $2 a week raise," he later said, "and sold 'em one share of stock each for $100, withholding the raise money to pay for the stock. So in fifty weeks, they had it paid out. *Everybody* working for the store was a stockholder. And that was a good thing for morale."

The corporation was subsequently reorganized in various ways. By 1980, Mr. George had reduced his personal share in the company to only four per cent. But stock ownership by associates remains a fundamental feature of the organization. Today, Publix is often referred to as the largest employee-owned company in the United States. Stock ownership is available to Publix associates in three ways:

1. The PROFIT Plan. The PROFIT plan is an employee stock ownership plan 100% funded by Publix. Publix has been annually contributing the equivalent of 9-11% of an eligible associate's earnings to the Plan, in the form of Publix stock.

2. The 401(k) plan. In addition to the PROFIT Plan, associates can invest in Publix stock through a 401(k) plan and receive a partial match in Publix stock.

3. The stock purchase plan. In 1959 Publix adopted an employee stock purchase plan, providing Publix associates (and *only* Publix associates) the right to purchase shares of

Publix stock. All active associates, whether full time or part time, and regardless of hours worked during the year, are eligible to purchase stock after a year of continuous employment.

Mark Hollis certainly thought that stock ownership was vital. Interviewed for that article mentioned earlier, Mark told the *New York Times*, "We would not have the same company if we didn't have employee ownership."

And Mr. George thought so. In explaining the motivation of Publix people in a speech at the University of Miami, Mr. George said, "We do offer our people more incentives than most other companies. Perhaps the two most important incentives are the profit-sharing plan and the stock ownership plan."

Having spent years listening to Publix people refer to "my" store or "my" company, I found it easy to imagine that ownership in the company – "owning a piece of the pie" – was the reason for Publix's success. Or if not *the* reason, at least the main ingredient in it. To this day, I *still* think that – but for different reasons than I once did.

The National Center for Employee Ownership (NCEO) reports the results of a study by professors Joseph Blasi and Douglas Kruse of Rutgers University, which found that sales at companies with employee stock ownership plans (ESOPs) grew 2.3% to 2.4% faster than would have been expected without an ESOP. The NCEO also describes an "Employee Ownership Index" (EOI) developed by Kruse, Blasi and Michael Conte of the University of Baltimore, which tracked stock prices of publicly traded companies with 10% or more employee ownership (and over fifty million dollars in market value). Their findings: from 1992 through 1997, the EOI group grew 193% while the Dow Jones Industrial Average was up only 145% and the Standard and Poors 500 only 140%.

From these studies, it seems that employee ownership can improve a company's performance. These studies provide good reason to think that's what happens at Publix. But the positive results of the Kruse and Blasi studies aren't uniform. After reviewing the results of thirty-one studies on the subject, Dr. Kruse points out that while some studies show employee ownership related to improved company performance, other studies fail to show any such correlation. Dr. Kruse concludes "there is clearly no *automatic* improvement of attitudes and behavior associated with being simply an employee-owner."[14]

And as we saw throughout Part One, superior customer service at Publix is not *directly* motivated by a desire for monetary reward. These behaviors are almost always the spontaneous result of common human kindness. So is there a relationship between stock ownership and kindness?

Yes there is. And it's because of how associate stock ownership at Publix is part of the company's culture.

As we've seen, Mr. George decided to start his own company while sitting outside his boss's office, after being told his boss was too busy to see him. *Alienation* from his boss – the feeling that his boss was one thing (too busy to talk to him), and that he was another (not worth an interruption for) – bothered him so much that he resolved to start a different kind of company.

"Right then I resolved that if I ever got to be a big shot in this business, two things would be done: I'd go around and visit the stores, and *if anybody wanted to see me they could walk into my office any time.*"

Mr. George was resolved to break down the wall between "boss" and "employee." Stock ownership at Publix is one of the fundamental ways of doing just that.

Every cashier, bagger, and custodial worker who works 1000 hours or more in a year becomes a Publix stockholder through the PROFIT plan. Those not yet eligible to buy stock soon will be, when they reach their first anniversary. The status of stockholder is something that *everyone* can relate to.

If only 10% of your company's employees are stockholders – say, by purchase of stock on the market, or through a 401(k) plan – then stock ownership isn't something you have in common with your co-workers.[15] But if stock ownership is spread across the

---

[14] NCEO website, http://nceo.org, accessed July 7, 2004.

[15] Data available on the NCEO website breaks down those who own stock in their companies by the employee's income level. The picture isn't surprising: it's the higher-ups in most companies who are more likely to own stock in their companies. Stock ownership at lower levels of employee compensation is relatively scarce. Less than six per cent of employees earning less than $15,000 a year report owning stock in their own companies.

entire workforce, as it is at Publix, then stock ownership is something that can be *assumed* among your co-workers. When *all or most* of your co-workers share that same sense of ownership, the dynamics get powerful. There's now a commonality, a sense of team.

But that's not all. Under the Publix stock purchase plan, if an associate wishes to sell his stock, the company has a right of first refusal to buy it back. So far, Publix has always done so. There is no market in Publix stock among the general public. As a practical matter, the only way a non-associate can acquire Publix stock is by gift or inheritance.[16] As a result, the vast majority of Publix stock is owned by Publix associates.

I've had people ask me how they can buy stock in Publix. When I explain that they can't, I can see the look of disappointment in their eyes. This is one of the many things that make being a Publix associate special. It sets Publix apart from other large companies often considered "employee-owned." Not only do almost all your co-workers own stock, but you're part of an *exclusive* group of people who can and do own stock.

Stock ownership creates an avenue in which associates can receive dividends. It's an investment which they can see grow. So it is a constant reminder of the connection between company success and individual success. But more than anything, it is the foundation for *identification of the individual with the group.*

Karl Marx described the *alienation* of workers from owners. Thorstein Veblen called workers "industrious" while calling business owners "predators" and "parasites." Frank Margiotta said customer service is the responsibility of management. Stephen Pollan urges people to "fire" their boss. Clearly, many today see the interests of owners and employees as adverse to each other.

But in a very real sense, putting stock in the hands of associates causes the interests of owners and employees to merge. It starts to break down the "we-they" mentality.

Barry Lewis is a typical Publix stockholder. He's been a full-time baker with Publix in St. Petersburg for ten years. Publix has contributed a significant amount (equivalent to 9-11% of his pay) to Barry's retirement plan every year. After ten years, Barry's PROFIT retirement account is now about twice his annual

---

[16] Or by becoming a member of the Board of Directors.

compensation. In addition, he purchases Publix stock through his 401(k).

Does being a stockholder make a difference to him?

"Absolutely," says Barry. "Owning stock in my company makes me feel like a million dollars!"

Why?

For one thing, Barry's Publix stock isn't just one item in a portfolio. Publix stock is *the* stock that Barry owns. It's his *only* company.[17]

When I asked Jim Rhodes why it was that he had gone so far as to scrub and polish the oven for the customer who'd let food build up in her oven, he replied, "Why did I clean that lady's oven? Because it was my company. Publix was looking out for my welfare, and I could do no less for it."

One final point about how widespread and exclusive stock ownership affects a company's culture: *the changes in attitude operate in two directions.*

I've focused primarily on how *being* an owner helps an associate identify with the company. But the second, and less apparent, effect of widespread associate ownership is its impact on managers, and how they *treat* these owners. Just as associate-owners are less likely to think of their manager as "the boss," managers are less likely to think of associate-owners as "just employees." With widespread and exclusive stock ownership, managers treat non-managers as the co-owners they are.

Just think about it: Don't managers always try to *please* their stockholders?

In its mission statement, Publix commits to be "dedicated to the dignity, value and employment security of our associates." Stock ownership helps Publix be not just a place where shopping is a pleasure, but where working is too. The two pleasures blend. As ingredients in the recipe, they combine almost chemically, one flavoring the other. Associate-owners get treated daily with the dignity that, at other companies, is too often reserved for major

---

[17] I'd be as quick as anybody to remind Barry about the benefits of diversification. But in the mean time, the fact that Publix is the *only* company Barry owns simply increases the extent to which Barry *identifies* with Publix.

stockholders.

So. It isn't just that Publix associates own stock. Or even that most of them own stock. It's the fact that, with rare exception for a few heirs and gift recipients, they're the *only* ones who own stock. It's the fact that this "exclusive club" sets them apart, and puts them all, store manager and cashier alike, together, on the same level at the top of the organization chart.

If you like acronyms, think of it as "We" thinking. That is, when stock ownership is both **W**idespread among employees and **E**xclusive to employees, it leads to thinking of the company as **WE**.

At Publix, stock ownership is the third ingredient in Publix's recipe for superior customer service. Giving better service will help the stock price rise, but that's not what motivates associate owners to give better service. It motivates associates because it causes associates to *identify,* and to *be* identified, with each other, and with what their company is all about.

As Ed Crenshaw says, speaking of his job as president among all the associates of Publix, "I'm the President of *their* company…"

No matter how routine they may seem to an associate, special occasions are always "special" to the customer. Here, when a bride decided she wanted a cake topper instead of flowers, Bakery Manager Cindy Osmer Lewis was at the reception making sure the customer was happy and "the sale was complete."

Publix Baker Vespasian Gayle shares a pie and a smile with a customer in Charleston, South Carolina.

24.
The Turbulent 90's

*G*rowing up in the Jenkins household, Mr. George's son Howard was steeped in the culture of Publix. He had started out bagging groceries for Publix in 1966. In January, 1990, with his father wheelchair-bound after his stroke, Howard became CEO. At that time, the company initiated a process of strategic planning. When it was over, Howard had decided to embark on what might be considered his biggest challenge as CEO: an aggressive campaign of expansion into new markets outside Florida.

In 1980, *Fifty Years of Pleasure* had reported the company's position on expansion outside Florida: namely, that it wasn't going to happen. The hauls would be too long from the centers of supply. The stores would be too far from headquarters for effective management. Customers outside Florida might have different tastes and expectations. And most of all, with a large, multi-state operation, how could Publix maintain the high standards of customer service it considered essential?

Everyone at Publix knew that expansion would not be easy. Ed Crenshaw talks about the first time he flew up to Atlanta. As he stood in the airport renting a car, the counter clerk who was serving him saw the name "Publix" on his credit card and asked him, "What is a Publix?"

Experts questioned how Publix could support its aggressive growth plans. The Company planned to approximately double in size during the 1990's. And not with mergers or acquisitions. New stores would have to be built by Publix from the ground up. Every new store manager, assistant store manager, department manager, and assistant department manager outside the Pharmacy would have to be trained and ready for promotion from within Publix. And while opening new stores out of state, Publix would continue to add stores within Florida. Altogether, new stores would have to be opened and staffed at the rate of one per week.

These obstacles all posed risks, but conviction strengthened that they could be overcome. By the beginning of the new decade, Publix was looking seriously at expanding outside of Florida. A great deal was at stake – the jobs and fortunes of tens of thousands of owners – but the risks stemming from expansion began to seem no bigger than the risks of sitting still.

Then, the decision was made. Publix began construction of its first non-Florida store in Savannah, Georgia, in April of 1991.

Not only were there people in Georgia who had never heard of Publix, there were others in that state who knew Publix well – and not all of them were interested in Publix's success. When Publix broke ground in Savannah, the company came to the attention not only of the other major supermarkets in the Atlanta market – like Kroger, A&P, Big Star and Cub Foods – but to the United Food and Commercial Workers Union (UFCW) as well. The opening of the Savannah store in November of 1991 went pretty much the same as several hundred openings before it had – with one exception: The UFCW launched a consumer boycott against Publix. People were standing at the entrances passing out flyers and handbills that urged customers not to shop at Publix. Among the charges: that Publix offered only low-paying, dead jobs.

But Publix's plans to open stores in Atlanta did not change. Publix opened four stores in the Atlanta area in late 1992. In 1993, it opened ten more stores in Georgia, and its first store in South Carolina. That year, Publix hired 48,551 new associates. And by the summer of 1994, Publix had over 30 stores in Georgia and South Carolina.

Would these new associates be able to deliver an environment where "shopping is a pleasure"? So much depended on people who had not grown up with Publix. People who didn't have years of exposure to "the Publix spirit." Was Publix's culture strong enough to remain focused on serving its new customers?

There were many factors that went into Publix's eventual success. But the one that most intrigued me was the decision to pay relocation bonuses to associates willing to move to new markets. Publix reimbursed moving expenses and paid relocation bonuses not only to managers, but to hourly-paid, non-management associates that other businesses might consider "unskilled." I was amazed. I'd never heard of a company doing that.

Of course, as Howard understood better than me, the point was that these people were *not* unskilled. They were Publix *example-setters*. They were Publix *story-tellers*. They were Publix *culture-builders*.

I'd been a Publix associate for little more than a year when Publix opened its first store in the Atlanta area. Store 33 opened in

Marietta on November 11, 1992. As the company's employment lawyer, I was there to observe and advise in case anything out of the ordinary happened.

By the time the store opened, there was a cold, steady rain. In a corner of the parking lot not covered by Publix's lease, news reporters and television cameras covered a press conference featuring UFCW vice president Frank Dininger. Dininger charged that Publix's "advertising claim of employee ownership is misleading" and sounded the theme of dead-end jobs.

The challenge went to the core of everything I'd seen and experienced at Publix.

Yet, despite the ugly weather outside, customers entered the store. They were smiling. Although every lane was open, there were still so many shoppers in the store that lines backed up into the grocery aisles. Many had been to Publix stores in Florida. They were saying how long they'd been waiting for Publix to come to Atlanta – and how delighted they were that the store was finally open. Publix associates returned the welcome with hospitality and equal enthusiasm.

Always the cautious, suspicious and cynical lawyer, I tried to remain distant. After all, I had a different job to do. But I found I couldn't resist. The enthusiasm of others grabbed me and wouldn't let me go. My dark blue suit made it obvious I was not a shopper. Customers kept coming up to me, telling me how happy they were with the store. Dropping all my privacy and reservation, I found myself talking to them, accepting their accolades on behalf of "my" company, and thanking them for their business.

Then, looking up at the rain pouring down, seeing them leave the covered walkway in front of the store with their umbrellas stretched open, I couldn't help but return their kindness. I remembered how Howard Jenkins had given me his umbrella on my first day at Publix. I started walking customers out to their cars, holding umbrellas over their heads. I even offered to take their keys and pull their cars up to the door so they wouldn't get wet.

I'd been bitten by the service mentality. My suit and my shiny black shoes were soaked, but my lawyer's heart – long stored in a courtroom deep freeze – seemed warmer than I ever remembered it.

It took a lot to penetrate the stuffed shirt I'd been wearing. But that day, I felt the pleasure of rendering service. I gleaned some of the good will that bounces back. More than anything else, overwhelmed by customer thanks, compliments, and good will, I

158

found myself proud of what I was doing and the people I was doing it with.

Other stores opened in the Atlanta area shortly thereafter. As the weeks went by, the customers kept coming. One day in Lakeland, Bill Sneed came into my office excited. "You'll never guess what the handbillers are doing now!" he said.

I went through the possibilities in my mind. Were they blocking customers from entering or exiting the stores? Engaging in sabotage? Had there been harsh words? Had the words led to fisticuffs?

"What are they doing?" I asked, expecting the worst.

Bill broke out in a smile.

"One of our store managers went out into the parking lot and offered them hot coffee," he said. "The next thing you know, they're coming into the store during their breaks to shop. They say the stores are great! Several of them have asked for jobs!"

According to the Shelby Report, which tracks market share in the supermarket industry, Publix's market share in the Atlanta area was 1.8 percent in August of 1993. By August of 1995, it had risen to 14 per cent.

Mike Chester, store manager in Kennesaw, tells of a day about a year after his store opened. It was extremely busy. A front-end associate approached him and said there was a customer who'd lost her keys somewhere in the store. The customer was distraught. Her young child was growing tired and adding to her frustration. Mike and others searched the store, looking for the lost keys, to no avail.

Eventually, someone thought to check the customer's car. Sure enough, the keys were still there, hanging in the ignition, locked inside the car.

Embarrassed, the customer couldn't believe the trouble she'd put the store to. Since the keys were locked in the car, Mike offered to have someone drive her home. The customer said she appreciated the offer, but she'd just like to come into the store and call her husband to come pick her up.

Mike brought her to the customer service desk. Offering to dial the number for her, he asked for her telephone number.

"Oh my gosh," said the customer. "I forgot. He's at work."

Mike asked her what the number was where her husband worked. She hesitated, and said she didn't know. Mike reached for the phone book and told her he would look the number up for her, and asked again where her husband worked.

By this time, the customer's embarrassment yielded only a grin. She leaned in close to Mike and said, "He's the manager of the Kroger on Jiles Road."

In July of 1996, Publix began opening stores in Huntsville, Alabama. By the end of 1997, there were 563 stores, including over a hundred outside of Florida. By the beginning of 2004, there were 805, including more than two hundred outside of Florida. According to the Shelby report, by the end of 2003, Publix had surpassed A&P, Cub Foods, Ingles, Harris Teeter and Winn Dixie in Atlanta. It had nearly 27 per cent of the market there – a close second behind Kroger (with 32 per cent).

Meanwhile, Publix had risen to 117th on the Fortune 500.

"We were smart," says Ed Crenshaw recently, looking back. "We made jobs in Atlanta available to anybody in Florida that wanted to relocate. We wanted to seed every store with as many experienced Publix associates as we possibly could, so that they could talk about George Jenkins and the history of the company and the philosophy of doing business, so we could transfer that knowledge to the new people we were hiring, so that they would know what makes this company successful. And I really think about how fortunate we were to have so many experienced people relocate up there."

Nearly ten years after I stood in the rain on opening day in Marietta, a customer I'll call Ms. M moved to Valdosta from North Carolina. Ms. M describes herself as "a single mom on a tight budget." She'd heard that Publix had good customer service, but she'd also heard that Publix's prices were higher than Wal-Mart's. So for two years, she stayed away from Publix. However, in January of 2004, she had a need of a Boars Head brand deli meat, and she heard she could only get it at Publix. So she drove to Publix. She had this to say in a letter to the company about the experience:

> After fighting for a parking place and wondering why on earth this place could possibly be so busy, I ventured in.
> First, the store is clean, attractive, and the layout is friendly to the handicapped. There were *several* motorized carts available, fully charged. I tooled around, taking in the

sights, then headed to the deli. Despite the large number of customers, I had no trouble getting through the spacious and uncluttered aisles. There was quite a crowd at the deli, and I was *astounded* at how friendly and respectful the deli-workers were. They did not seem rushed or annoyed at all and indeed, they seemed to *enjoy* their jobs!

The gentleman who helped me was polite, kind and respectful. He offered me a sample of the new "Blazing Buffalo Chicken," which I accepted. I found it too spicy for my taste. When I commented that it was too hot, he asked if I'd like some water, then proceeded to come out from behind the counter and get some water for me!

As I continued to shop, I was offered many samples (so nice!) I asked to speak to a manager. I tried to convey just how happy I was with my shopping experience. You see, I am afflicted with crippling arthritis that makes standing on my feet to shop virtually impossible. It has been my experience in other stores that people in motorized carts or wheelchairs are often overlooked because they are not at eye-level. I am also morbidly obese, which often garners me less than acceptable service, as some people have great disdain for the obese, and don't hesitate to show it.

I was fighting back tears as I tried to tell the manager what a positive experience I had in her store. This may seem a tad melodramatic, but I guess unless you've been in this situation, it's hard to understand just how disheartening it can be to have people look past you all the time. In your store, I felt valued, respected and appreciated.

I'm sending my teenage son to apply for a job at Publix tomorrow. Any company who has such positive, happy employees *must* treat them well!

Thank you, Publix. You have won this customer over for GOOD!

L.M.
Valdosta, Georgia

25.
Pride

*G*eorge Jenkins once said, "We have a society today where, for the most part, people's basic needs are taken care of. But people are looking for something more, and that something has to do with their relationship with *themselves*. You can call it self-respect or self-esteem or individualism; but whatever you call it, it is, I believe, the key to motivation of most people today."

More recently, Miami store manager Ozzie Lopez told this story:

While working in the produce department at Store 94, Ozzie was approached by a customer with a complaint about a three pound bag of onions that were rotten. The customer said she'd never seen such terrible product in her life. Ozzie agreed, saying the onions should never have been sold to her, and he got a fresh three pound bag, which he gave to the woman free of charge.

In a pattern we've already encountered, it was only then that Ozzie pointed out one more thing: the bag of onions she'd first brought in had been purchased at a competitor's store.

The customer apologized, thanked Ozzie repeatedly, not wanting to accept a free replacement for a competitor's product. When Ozzie insisted, the customer told him that Publix had a customer for life.

What makes this story different from other, similar stories is what happened next. As the customer left, *another* customer approached Ozzie, having *witnessed* what had just transpired.

"Publix didn't just gain a customer for life," said the second customer. "It gained two." And with that, the second customer, who normally didn't buy onions, picked up a three pound bag of onions for himself.

Think about that. I'm convinced it reveals the final ingredient in how to get employees to give superior customer service.

The second customer in this story witnessed something he believed was special. Something that was extraordinary. And he wanted, somehow, to be a part of it.

That, I believe, is the key. In that simple respect, there's no difference between customers and employees. No difference between firemen and faculty members, carpenters and construction workers, sanitation workers or sales clerks.

It's human nature to want to be a part of something that's good.

It's not the logical, calculating, *"If I give superior performance, my stock price will go up."*

Rather, it's the emotional, *"It makes me feel good to be a part of something extraordinary."*

Widespread and exclusive stock ownership is the foundation for associates to identify with Publix. But as we consider the matter of identification with the company, we have to consider, at the same time, the matter of *pride.*

In "Your Associate Handbook," given to every new associate, the very first words one reads inside the cover are, from Charlie Jenkins Jr., CEO, "Welcome to the Publix Family. You are now part of the best food and drug retailer in the United States."

A powerful statement. Even though it's based on neutral studies and objective national polls, some might even call it arrogant. But whether it's true or not, Publix begins its relationship with new associates proclaiming that it's so.

Welcome to our family.

You're now part of *the best.*

It's a direct appeal to pride.

There are, however, two parts to pride. And when everything's working as it should, Publix associates feel both. There's pride in oneself, and there's pride in the organization.

Let's take those one at a time. First, pride in oneself. When everything's going as it should, associates don't feel they're just cogs in a wheel, but valued and important parts of something extraordinary.

As we saw early on, one of the things heard most often at Publix is Mr. George's statement, "Publix will be a little better place, or not quite as good ... because of you." The associate is reminded often of his or her importance. He or she is a stockholder. He or she has the power to make a difference.

Publix associate Gerry Talbert says, "When I first started with Publix in the early 1970's, it was not unusual to see Mr. George doing some grocery shopping at the Publix Wabash Shopping Center across from the former corporate offices. On more than one occasion, I would actually see Mr. George bag a customer's groceries, especially if the store was busy."

Gerry isn't alone. I heard again and again from Publix associates how they had *personally* seen Mr. George walk into a

163

store and start bagging customers' groceries. He was continually visiting the stores, mingling with associates and customers alike. He loved to be out, talking to people. And he kept on doing it even when he was the head of a company with over a billion dollars in sales each year.

People have often said he did it because he loved interaction with customers. I feel certain that's true. But I believe he had another reason as well: the example it set for Publix associates. And I'm not talking about a demonstration of proper bagging technique. He knew that others could teach people not to put a twenty-pound turkey on top of a loaf of bread.

Rather, I think he was demonstrating something about the *value* of bagging groceries. Worth many millions of dollars, Mr. George was showing that he wasn't too good, or too rich, or too "important" to bag groceries. If *he* could take the time to smile and chat while bagging groceries for a single customer, it said something not only about the importance of that customer, but the importance of the job. That job was pure customer service. And customer service was, in fact, what made Publix what it was. So he was *proud* to do it.

Service, by its nature, is a matter of placing the needs of somebody else above your own. For many people in these selfish times, a "service" mentality is too much for the ego to handle. And of all the jobs in a supermarket, bagging groceries has often been thought of as an unattractive job. But if a multi-millionaire like George Jenkins could be proud to bag groceries, why couldn't anyone else?

And he even seemed to enjoy it! What an impact that example, repeated often, must have had over the years! Performing the simplest task with pride and a smile. Embracing the service mentality. The man probably turned to more than one associate as he left the store -- after commenting about the latest price of Publix stock, to the fellow-stockholder beside him -- by repeating: "Publix will be a little better place, or not quite as good ... because of you."

Consider this e-mail by John Coppock, a cashier at Store 540 in LaGrange:

> About one month ago I was approached by one of my customers. She apologized for bothering me but she said she knew I would help her.
>
> I quickly said, 'You are never a bother to me,' and 'What is it I can do for you?'

She needed some frozen beans that were all the way to the back of the top shelf in the freezer and she could not reach them. We walked to the freezer. I could barely reach the item myself (we got a chuckle out of that) but in the end, I was able to get the beans down for her.

I take great pride and pleasure in helping my customers whenever and however I can.

Asked why she goes out of her way for customers, Fort Lauderdale store manager Ursula Eivers says, "I take great pride when I hear a customer refer to the store as '*my*' Publix."

One thing that contributes to pride is the appreciation one so often hears from customers. Wendy Jones, an office associate in Nashville, describes how "a chance presented itself to make the Publix impact" on a customer when a customer's car wouldn't start. Wendy called AAA, drove the customer to the groomer to get her puppy, and then drove the customer home.

"The customer thanked me numerous times and called me her angel," says Wendy. "That comment alone made my day, and also made me realize that although things like this don't happen every day, I'm able to make an impact in much smaller ways. Many of this customer's friends have now started shopping at Publix, thanking us for the care we gave her and mentioning what wonderful customer service we have."

Andrew Drayton is a meat cutter on Daniel Island. He describes how a customer came in wanting to know how many pounds of rib eye roast she needed to feed nine people. He took delight in explaining, detail by detail, the factors to consider, including whether it was boneless or bone-in, desired portion size, and so on. He describes how the customer wanted it on a Saturday, and how he worked on Saturday, and so "I would personally prepare it myself."

Then, "Two days later I received a call from the customer and she seemed overjoyed with the outcome of her dinner. About a week later, my store manager gave me a copy of the letter that corporate wrote to her. I also received a gold coin in recognition for my outstanding customer service. I guess I just love what I do."

Positive feedback from customers and managers can be a powerful motivator, by stimulating the pride a person feels. When an associate develops not just sales, but genuine *relationships*, the opportunity for positive feedback from customers increases.

Lee Gramm in Atlanta remembers getting a letter from a

customer who reported the sad news that his wife had passed away. But the customer went on to describe how his wife "had often talked to her family and friends about the nice young man from Publix who helped her home one day." It had been two years since Lee had helped the woman, yet her husband was still appreciative enough to write a thank you to the store.

"I never felt so touched or proud that day to be a Publix associate," said Lee.

Pride in one's job – stimulated by customer appreciation and recognition from management – is an essential ingredient in customer service at Publix. But it's not just pride in one's own job that's important. As said earlier, there is also pride in each other, and in the organization.

Because of the sense of team, and identification with the organization that comes from "WE" stock ownership, associates take pride in each other. In Duluth, for over a year, an elderly gentleman who is blind has called Store 726 every Friday. Store personnel take his order and one of the associates shops for him.

"He raves about our customer service," says Brandy Burley, administrative coordinator. "He says he couldn't get this kind of service anywhere else. We always try to help, any way we can. *That's what makes us different.*"

Consider what store manager Dale Fields sent me about Jay Tokash, a young Publix associate who sadly passed away in February, 2004, at the age of 24. Dale says there was an outpouring of grief from associates and customers alike.

"A minimum of three hundred customers either came to customer service or stopped a manager in the store to let us know that they were truly sorry that Jay had passed away. There were even a couple of dozen customers at Jay's funeral. Each customer told us how Jay seemed to be the life of the store. Every time they came in, Jay greeted them with a smile on his face and took care of all of their needs. They said they never saw him have a bad day. Many customers sent cards to the family. Others wanted to help out financially. The overwhelming support his family received from our customers was amazing. Many to this day still mention how they miss him. It just goes to show how one person can make a difference in the lives of others."

Then, wrote Dale, "One question will sum up this letter. How many people do you know at other retailers that YOU would miss if they were to suddenly pass away?"

I hear sadness, there, to be sure. But also, a *pride* in Jay Tokash. A pride so strong that Dale couldn't keep it down if he tried.

Lisa Nichols was a brand new Publix associate when she wrote to the corporate office that she'd seen store manager Tim Bismarck out in the parking lot, loading a customer's groceries. As a new associate, she said, it inspired her.

"I came to work for Publix 11 years ago," wrote Brenda Dunn. "I have many memories, but one of my favorites is of a former store manager named Mike Shannon. It was several years ago on a rainy Saturday and our store was very busy. As customers would exit with their carts of groceries, Mike took control, telling them to go get their car and drive up. He worked all day in the rain, loading customers' groceries. Cars were lined across the front of the store. The scene brought tears to many eyes.

"One customer asked, 'Who is that man?'"

"I explained proudly, 'He is my store manager.'"

Referring to the importance Publix attaches to developing relationships, store manager Brek Williams says, "I realized that this is the part of Publix that makes us so special. The reason why I am proud to work here."

You may recall from Chapter 7 Holly Lowe's description of her experience in the warehouse just before Thanksgiving. "I'd never witnessed such an unselfish act of teamwork before," she says. "I was *so proud* to be a part of it."

Or Joanne Mullery's description of the day the people mover broke down in Miami Beach. "The way our entire store jumps in and takes care of business, it makes me proud to be part of Store 73 and Publix."

Or what happened when Barbara Murray raved to the front service clerk about his manager, and the clerk responded, "That's nothing," followed by a story of even better service by that manager.

What is it that makes an associate *brag* about his store manager's customer service?

Pride.

"Our team knows we're in the service business," says Todd Jones. "I love to see the reactions of customers when we go above and beyond. Publix people are *proud of our reputation*. We are never embarrassed to tell others who we work for, because our company realizes that *people* are the reason for our success."

The immediate reward that a person receives for an act of

service or kindness is the direct motivator. But pride in what you do, and in the organization with which you're identified as you do it, drives people to take it one step further, and to repeat it, and to excel at it.

There's one more thing about pride: Success is not its most essential ingredient.

Lawyers as a group have accumulated large amounts of wealth; they make up a majority of Congress; they may have more influence in the election of Presidents than any other special interest group in the country. By almost any definition, lawyers are successful. Yet we are the butt of jokes and at times the object of genuine scorn.

That day in Marietta, on the other hand – the day I helped customers out to their cars in the rain – I felt something I wasn't used to at all. I felt appreciated. It was a feeling I'd rarely experienced, and I basked in it. I'd felt prouder than I'd ever felt as a lawyer. Because lawyers – whether they deserve it or not – are not, generally, viewed as *good*.

People want to be identified with something that's not only successful, but *good*. It's the most important ingredient in feeling proud about who you are and what you do.

Success breeds energy and motivation. Success may even result in a measure of pride. But no matter how good people feel about their own efforts, and their own performance, how many people can feel proud to be part of a *bad* organization?

A key ingredient in Publix's *customer* service, therefore, is its record in *community* service. Its record of *doing the right thing* means that the spirit of service is, at the same time, the spirit of doing good.

Publix people don't just hear compliments from others about the job they've done personally. They don't just hear raves about their co-workers and the company's reputation for providing good customer service. They hear from non-customers, expressing thanks for the many ways in which Publix contributes to the community. The United Way. The March of Dimes. Refreshments for firefighters. Water and ice during hurricanes. Working with schools or local charities. Being involved in the Girl Scouts, or in Big Brothers/Big Sisters, or in Little League.

Pride in the individual contribution you make, regardless of the job you hold. Pride in your team mates. Pride in your organization.

The most important ingredient of all.

26.
The Recipe

So. "How can I get my employees to treat the public this way?"
Those in marketing or the media might say that the most important thing is to communicate the strategy well. They might point out the importance of choosing a few key principles that describe the company's focus, and then turning them into slogans that everyone can relate to. Consider how central to the stories in this book are just five simple expressions of Publix philosophy:

- "Publix, where shopping is a pleasure."
- "No sale is complete until the meal is eaten and enjoyed."
- "Publix will be a little better place, or not quite as good... because of you."
- "Dedicated to the dignity, value, and employment security of our associates."
- "Involved as responsible citizens in our communities."

Those five quotations sum it all up very well. But a letter from one customer, while expressing regrets about having to move away from the states in which Publix does business, gave me an idea for a different way to sum it all up.

First, the letter:

Now, my family and I are leaving Florida and moving to Illinois. I will greatly miss shopping at Publix. The associates are always so friendly and helpful, and I'm always able to find what I need. My children love shopping at Publix with me. In their play, my girls always pretend to "run errands" and "stop at Publix." My two year old associates the letter P with Publix. Every time she says a letter P, she says, "It's Publix, Mommy!"

I will miss your store greatly. Thank you for your great service.

M. L.
Satisfied customer for 8 years

Personally, I think the little girl has something there. One way to summarize and remember the Publix recipe might be with the following nine P's:

1. People. Nearly all people are *capable* of rendering great customer service. But some of them have a *desire* to serve customers, while others do not. Hire people who have the desire. It will soon become clear who has the desire and who does not. Through self-selection, those who desire to serve are the ones who will stay.

2. Pleasure. Once the team is assembled, it's all about creating the conditions under which associates' natural kindness will blossom. Make clear that the most important thing is to please the customer. Then remember that genuine, caring service can't be faked. People are basically good; in the right environment, they'll do good things for each other.

3. Power. Recognize the difference between satisfying customers and delighting them. Delighting them requires exceeding their expectations. That means you've got to listen to what the customer really cares about. Also, to create delight, to exceed expectations, people must be empowered to "break the rules" of doing only what's expected. Make clear that "doing the unexpected" is what *is* expected. Get people to ask themselves, "If we *can* do it, then why not?"

4. Practice. For delight and the unexpected to become common, there must be practice and reinforcement. The best leadership comes from examples. Examples that are seen, and examples that are talked about. All it takes to begin a relationship is a glance, a smile, a thank you. Be observant. Be alert. There are opportunities to begin relationships everywhere. Take advantage of them. Practice, and set the example.

5. Praise. When people do well, give them recognition. Celebrate the occasions when people give great service. Tell stories!

6. Promote from within. Once you've got a good thing going, promoting from within is a great way to keep those examples coming. It gives new people something to look forward to, and it ensures they'll be surrounded by people with lots of examples and stories to tell. It enables the manager to do the jobs the new people are doing, and so makes setting examples (and feeling pride) much easier.

7. Proprietary interest. Give people not only a financial stake in the outcome, but a real basis for identifying with the organization. "Widespread and exclusive" stock ownership is Publix's way of emphasizing each associate's identification with the group, and with the organization. In its absence, there must be some other way to reinforce identification of the individual with the rest of the team.

8. Pride in the job. Recognize the value of every job, especially those that deal directly with customers. Demonstrate the importance of each one. If a manager won't do the job, why should a new clerk consider it important?

9. Pride in the organization. Make certain that the organization itself always does the right thing, that it sets an example of being a responsible corporate citizen. And make sure that employees are aware of the good things the organization does for the community. If the organization demonstrates its own commitment to service, people will want to be a part of it. People want to be a part of something extraordinary.

How's *that* for a purple potato perspective?

27.
What's In Store

Now in its 75th year, Publix is poised to start another quarter century – the beginning of an approach to its hundredth birthday.

As it does so, there are many signs of continuing growth and success. Publix is in five states. Its business in the Atlanta market has grown, surpassing twenty percent of the market share there. Through the "Apron's" program, Publix is expanding its involvement in quick food preparation and "meal solutions." Publix has recently increased its investment in Crispers, bringing a healthful salad and sandwich business into the store. On August 1, 2004, Publix's stock price hit another all time high at $58.50 per share.

But other things have not changed. A letter to Charlie Jenkins, Jr., the CEO, pretty well captures it all:

> My wife and I, and our entire family including two small grandchildren, shop at Publix several times a week. We would like to tell you what a joy it is to shop at your stores.
>
> We feel it is like walking into a friendly, safe, familiar environment. Here, the best selection of food and outstanding fresh produce can be found. We find the employees to be extremely helpful, happy and caring. The stores are super clean and the atmosphere is upbeat. You have assistance to your car with all the packages.
>
> It's always a treat to try tasty new food ideas by enthusiastic food servers. Some of our neighbors work there and have made the store part of their family. You accommodate us even when we need a "last minute" party platter or a special coke. Our daughter joined the Baby Club. It is a great community service for our little ones and their parents. Publix gives job opportunities to individuals that are physically or mentally challenged, which gives a needed job and self-esteem to that person.
>
> For all the positive reasons above, I am sure Publix will grow into other states. "Publix is for the public." I am sure

your uncle who started the store in 1930 would be very proud of you for carrying on his vision.

Mark and Diane Nathan
Sarasota, Florida

What a nice letter, and what a nice thought.

But there's one factor that looms in Publix's future like no other. And that's Wal-Mart.

Wal-Mart is bigger than General Motors. Bigger than General Electric. Bigger than ExxonMobil. It does more business than Target, Sears, Kmart, J.C. Penney, Safeway and Kroger combined. It has well over a million employees, and it has sales that will almost certainly soon exceed *three hundred billion* dollars in a year. It's nearly twenty times the size of Publix. In the mere handful of years since it entered the food business, its market share has sky-rocketed to first place in Alabama, Louisiana, South Carolina, Mississippi, and Tennessee. In Georgia and Kentucky, it is second only to Kroger. In North Carolina it is second only to Food Lion. And in Florida, it is close to overtaking Winn-Dixie in the second spot, behind Publix. As of 2004, there was a Wal-Mart Super Center within five miles of half of Publix stores.

Against the Wal-Mart powerhouse, will the factors identified in the Nathans' letter be enough? Will the things that brought Publix this far be enough for the Publix family of associate-owners to succeed for another twenty-five years, and more?

Here's an e-mail from Mableton, Georgia, one of those many locations where Wal-Mart has a Super Center:

> My husband and grandchildren require no-sugar-added or sugar-free products. We have shopped at Kroger or the Wal-Mart Superstore for the last twenty years. Both stores discontinued the Nestle no-sugar-added powdered chocolate mix. We have not been happy with either of these stores for quite a while. I went to Publix and ordered our Thanksgiving meal and then asked Ms. Jenni Young, night store manager, if they could get the chocolate mix.
>
> She stopped what she was doing and checked her computer, but could not locate it. She asked me to go home and call her back with the UPC number, which I did. She called back and said she could order it, and did for us. When I went to the store yesterday I was able to buy five boxes with a promise from Ms. Young that she would make

sure it was on the shelf.

My husband and I will be doing our shopping at Publix from now on. Everybody at the Mableton Walk store are so friendly and ask if we need help. You got new customers. Thank you, Publix and Ms. J. Young.

Susan Poirier
Mableton, Georgia

Says Julia Lehr of Store 300 in Tampa, "With a Wal-Mart Super Center right around the corner, they think they're giving us a run for our money. But it's our customers giving Wal-Mart the run. As our customers are checking out, they make it a point to let us know how friendly all associates are here in the store, how the shelves are stocked to their liking, and how our service is top rate. Most have mentioned while in Wal-Mart, their associates aren't friendly and don't help the customer. That's what makes us a pleasure to shop with!"

At Store 882 in Birmingham, Alabama, a customer came into the store in April, 2004 to order a cake. Manager Derrick Holden approached to see if she was being taken care of. When she asked if he knew of a location close by where she could order a Pizza to go, Derrick not only told her of a place, but asked one of his associates to look up the number for her in the phone book, so she could order the pizza before she left the store.

The customer was impressed. When she came in the next day for her cake, she told Derrick she and her husband had discussed the great service at Publix and they hoped there'd be a Publix in her area soon – so they could shop at Publix, rather than Wal-Mart.

Katie Combs works at the Publix in Flowery Branch, Georgia. One evening, she got a call from an elderly patient at the Northeast Georgia Medical Center in Gainesville. (The patient had gotten Katie's name from Katie's sister, who works at the Center.) The lady explained that she was at the hospital with her husband, and wasn't able to go home to feed the dog. She wanted to know if someone could bring some dog food to the hospital. Katie agreed to do so and hung up.

Then she began wondering how the lady would be able to feed her dog if she couldn't leave the hospital.

"I called her back," says Katie. "I offered to take the dog food to her house. I got directions and took the dog food. The dog was in the back yard and was very excited when he finally got fed."

The dog wasn't the only one well pleased.

"The lady was very grateful," says Katie. "Now she drives twelve miles to shop at our store, when she used to shop at Wal-Mart."

Mark Pittman passed along this e-mail from Tim Bryant, store manager in Crestview:

> One evening we had a customer come in to our store and she was in a panic. She needed to have some cupcakes and a birthday cake made up. She said she had just come to us from Wal-Mart. She was upset because they refused her order. They said she did not give them enough notice. She came into our store and was hoping not to get the same response, because she needed it at 7 a.m. the next morning and it was 9:30 p.m.
>
> Our decorator was working late that night and she was more than happy to take the order and assured the customer it would be done when she needed it. The customer could not believe how friendly our associate Marlyn Schultz was, and the fact she was willing to do whatever it took to get the cake ready.
>
> The customer came in the next day and her comment was that she wouldn't ever get a cake from Wal-Mart again.

Ed Crenshaw was talking recently about the original leaders of Publix -- George and Charlie Jenkins, Joe Blanton, Pete Newsome, Charlie Capps and others like them. He pointed out that they had built the company into what it is today. Then he turned to the job facing the current generation of Publix leaders.

"Our job," he said, "is to make sure that we adapt as the environment around us changes, but at the same time, to remain faithful to what sets us apart. So many of those basics that the early leaders taught us will *always* apply. Regardless of how much the business changes, there are some of those basics, like the attention to the customer, and the way we want to treat the associates in the company – those are things that don't change at all. And that's the reason I believe that Publix will be a strong healthy company for many, many years to come. Because that work ethic is there, the culture is there, the philosophy of doing business – it's there. And it's in so many people.

"In spite of all the changes that have gone on around us, the customer hasn't changed," says Ed. "They're willing to pay a reasonable price for good service, and to reward a company with their business if they do get good service. Our future lies in our reputation for service. That's the way we're going to succeed. That's the great vision that George Jenkins had in 1930 – providing great customer service. It hasn't changed.

"Publix has been successful, and will continue to be successful, because of what George Jenkins instilled in us. It's a people business. We'll only be successful as a result of people: our associates and our customers. And we will continue to be successful in the future if we continue to treat people the way they want to be treated. By employing associates that enjoy serving people. Treating them with the dignity and respect that we talk about. And because of our customers that enjoy shopping in an environment where people care about them. Where they receive the value for the product and services that they purchase in our stores.

"That's just not the supermarket business. That's *any* business. It's how well you get along with people. And as I think about it, George Jenkins is the one that instilled that in me.

"I'm amazed that more businesses don't understand that. Because it's not difficult to understand that it's all about people, and relationships, and how you interact and communicate with each other. The people who do that the best, to me, are the ones that are the most successful. Either collectively, as a company, or as individuals. It's all about people."

I'll end with a final customer letter. This one's from Paul Schorkopf of Brentwood, Tennessee:

> We have recently moved to Tennessee from New Jersey and have been trying to get our bearings in a new town. My wife had decided to make her famous scalloped oysters for Christmas and had called our local supermarket to order three pints of oysters. I was dispensed to pick up said special order on Christmas Eve around one o'clock.
>
> When I got there a nice young man said indeed our order was ready. But when he brought them out, a mishap occurred and two of the pints went smashing to the floor. I struggled to maintain my composure and asked him if there were any more oysters to be had. Sadly, that was the last of the store's stock.

I stood there trying to figure out what to do when the store manager, Joe Zarcone, approached me and asked me if there was a problem. I explained what had happened and he asked me to wait while he went to get the meat manager, Ed Parker. Mr. Parker heard my sad tale and asked me for my address. He said that he would call his other stores in the area, find the oysters, and deliver them to my house!

His exact words when I protested that I would be glad to come and pick them up were, 'Please, sir, it's no problem. I'd be glad to do it. Christmas is too stressful as it is.' I walked away stunned. Sure enough, two hours later, they were delivered by Mr. Parker to my house!

But wait: there's more! I bumped into Mr. Parker three days later and went to shake his hand to say thanks, again. I asked him how far he'd had to go to get the oysters. He said he had called every Publix store within a 25 mile radius, only to find that all the stores were out of oysters. I asked him how he'd gotten the oysters, and his answer nearly floored me! He had called every store of every supermarket chain in the area until he found one that had the oysters. He then went there on his own, purchased the oysters from a competitor and delivered them to my family!

But wait: there's more! Not only did he buy oysters for my order, but on the chance that someone else might need them, he bought the rest of that store's stock (25 pints) and brought them to his store so that he would not be caught short taking care of other customers' needs on Christmas eve! Amazingly, he sold out the remaining oysters by 6:30 that night!

Not only have you earned a customer for life, with a tale that will be told and retold by me, but one man took time out in this all too dreary world to bring an extra measure of kindness to one who did not expect it, but will never forget it. Mr. Parker and Mr. Zarcone are a testament to the kind of employees that Publix attracts and keeps, the corporate credo and managerial standards that Publix sets and maintains; the reason why Publix will flourish as others wither away. Being in sales and public relations, I wish that I had one person like Mr. Parker, with that sense of duty, pride in brand and deeply held conviction to serve and be proud of who he is and what he represents. If I had ten like him I would rule the world!

So there is my Christmas tale. I hope you will pass it on to those who may in some small way return some of the kindness and certainly recognize the quality of your wonderful employees.

Paul Schorkopf
Brentwood, Tennessee

About the Author

Joe graduated from the Phillips Exeter Academy and from the University of Pennsylvania with a degree in English. In 1971 he became director of human resources at a manufacturing company in south Florida; while working days, he went to law school at night at the University of Miami. Thereafter, Joe represented business clients on issues of employment and human resources law and was a frequent speaker on those subjects. In 1992, Joe joined Publix Super Markets as human resources counsel; in 1998, he was elected vice president of human resources and employment law at Publix.

Throughout his human resources and legal career, Joe maintained an active interest in writing. While at Publix he published his first book, and at the end of 2003, he retired from Publix in order to devote more time to that avocation.

Joe and his wife of thirty two years have four children and a grandchild.

Other Books by the Author:

Now available:

Cage Stories: Memories of Fatherhood and Creation
A collection of true stories. Morris Publishing. © 2000

and

Once in the Master's House
Historical fiction. (The Roman Empire, first century a.d.)
© 2005

Available soon:

A Conspiracy to Kill
Historical fiction. (The plot to assassinate Nero.)

Contact the author on the web at jwcarvin.com
or by e-mail at jwcarvin@aol.com